Faith in Action

Medical Missionaries in Central America

The story of Central American Medical Outreach in photographs and prose.

—

Narrator, Mike Billington ~ Cari DeSantis, Photographer

WHITE ROSE BOOKS
HOCKESSIN, DELAWARE

Design by Teresa Ewald, Ewaldesign.

ISBN #0-9660486-0-1

WHITE ROSE BOOKS
30 CLARK RIDGE
HOCKESSIN, DELAWARE
19707-1516
U.S.A.

Printed in the United States of America on recycled paper.

Contents

Acknowledgments

We wish to acknowledge the contributions of the many CAMO volunteers who allowed us to photograph and interview them during the course of this project and whose special gifts brought hope and life to a forgotten people on a forgotten isthmus south of these United States. A special thanks to Kathy Tschiegg, founder and executive director of Central American Medical Outreach (CAMO) for allowing us to tell this story in pictures and words, for her constant encouragement and prayers, and for believing that one person can make a difference and showing us all how.

We wish to also acknowledge our new-found friends in Honduras, the medical and dental caregivers who do so much with so little to help their countrymen and women in need and who work hard along with the CAMO volunteers to improve the standard of care in their country. A special acknowledgment must go to Gladys Castellanos, the director of nursing in Hospital de Occidente de Santa Rosa de Copán and CAMO liaison in Honduras. Her good nature and sense of humor endear her to all who meet her and are surpassed only by her dedication and commitment to proper medical care for the poor in her country.

And to the people of Honduras, who came to us for hope, but gave us so much more in return. They taught us how faith and love bridge all language barriers.

A special thanks to Anabis Vera-Gonzalez, M.D. for her assistance with translations and medical terminology throughout this book and for her friendship.

One final acknowledgment from Cari: a special thanks to my children Cory and Anna Rose for patience and encouragement throughout this book project and for your understanding of the weeks I have spent in Honduras - weeks away from you. They say we teach best by example. My prayer is that you, too, will seek to serve those less fortunate throughout your lives.

Mike Billington
Cari DeSantis

Forward

Three days she walked, this mother with child, to reach Santa Rosa in time. Three days her sandaled feet padded along the soft brown dirt on narrow trails leading over mountains, through streams and valleys, dense foliage and fear. Three days with Carmencita balanced on her left hip. A ragged bundle of meager food on her right. A constant, fervent prayer on her lips. Three days she walked, on faith alone, that the 'gringos', the "medicos de la brigada" would fix her baby's face, so the child could live a normal life.

Carmencita is her baby, the youngest of seven children. Barely two, she had been born with severe deformities: cleft lip, cleft palette and a facial tumor that worsened as she grew and marked her forever as an outcast from the village society, a child of the devil. In a country so fervent in its Christian faith, superstition yet dies hard. Lydia prayed to a merciful God. And then word came about ***La Brigada.***

La brigada. The brigade. The medical teams of Central American Medical Outreach (CAMO), an Ohio-based non-profit organization of volunteer medical missionaries: doctors, nurses and support personnel, who use hard-earned vacation time from their regular jobs, pay their own airfare and expenses and endure third world living conditions and heart-breaking scenes to make a difference in the lives of the poorest of the poor in a hemisphere that holds untold riches.

I first became aware of CAMO in January 1994, when a social worker who joined the team as a translator was featured in the employee newsletter at the hospital where we both worked. At the time, I filed away the article for the future, perhaps when my kids were grown or I had more vacation time. One year later, I came across that article and called.

I spoke with Kathy Tschiegg, CAMO founder and executive director. I was impressed by her story: former Peace Corps Volunteer, currently a trauma nurse in a big city hospital Emergency Room, faith-filled Christian with a fierce determination to improve the dismal quality of medical care she witnessed during her time in Central America. Kathy founded CAMO in 1993 and began a journey of faith, of hope and, above all, of love.

I was mightily impressed with the CAMO philosophy, which is based on the old adage; *give a man a fish and he eats for a day; teach a man to fish and he eats for life.* That makes CAMO unique: CAMO not only provides much needed surgical and medical intervention, but also the tools and the education the Honduran medical personnel need to carry-on the healing far beyond the team's stay.

The implications of that philosophy of medical missionary work are so far reaching...and so remarkable.

Two weeks in Honduras in 1995 convinced me that this story must be told. It is a love story of the greatest kind. The story of a love that calls ordinary people to put their faith in action and so answer the words of Jesus Christ: *...whatsoever you shall do for the least of my brothers and sisters, that you do unto me.*[1]

The volunteers come from the heartlands of Ohio, from the mesas of Arizona, from the suburbs of Detroit, from the everglades of Florida and the financial centers of Delaware. From Virginia, New Jersey, California, Pennsylvania and Washington D.C. From sixteen states (so far) and Puerto Rico. They come to Santa Rosa de Copán, Honduras, Central America. An unremarkable, very poor country across the Gulf from Texas.

They are doctors and nurses, dentists and technicians, biomedical engineers, anesthesiologists, respiratory and physical therapists, x-ray techs and mammography techs. They are hearing specialists, opthamologists, translators, drivers, and people whose strong arms are needed to load equipment, move supplies and hug frightened children. They are of all creeds and races, of varied educational backgrounds and economic circumstances. Most have never met before; most cannot speak Spanish; yet they come together for a common goal: There is a need and they can help meet it.

What is it that calls these people from all over the country to gather with dozens of strangers to serve far from home, helping people they do not know and may never see again? How is it that these few are chosen to come together in service to peoples unknown, then drift back to their everyday middle class American lives forever touched by the knowledge that they made a difference? Some return year after year; others do not. And what of those back home who do not venture to the highlands, but give their time, their dollars and their prayers. *Blessed are they that have not seen and yet have believed.*[2]

I have pondered these questions ever since I first witnessed CAMO teams in action in early 1995. Perhaps the answers do not matter. But this I do know: they ask no reward, no recognition, no glory. They do it because it must be done. *If not me, then who?*

They endure a full day of travel, followed by a three-hour torturous mountain climb in a rattletrap bus to reach Santa Rosa. They start each day at 6:30 a.m. and often work until 8 or 9 at night, then hope for a hot shower, or a cold shower, or any water at all to wash off the dust and the absolute poverty they've been immersed in all day, resume their work the next day and the next, for a week or two or, for some, three. They eagerly bridge the language barrier with volunteer translators to impart to their Honduran counterparts the knowledge they have acquired working in the world's best health care system, knowing that, more often than not, these Honduran nurses and doctors must simply stand by and watch people die or suffer horrible pain or permanent disfigurement for the lack of a single piece of equipment, enough anesthesia, antibiotics or adequate preventive care. There is so much to do and so little time and *what are they among so many?*

The biggest challenge for the volunteers is not the long hours nor the hard work, but the frustration...despair...and the urge to cry over the unfairness of it all.

But this is not a tragedy, this is a story of hope. Although at times it appears that what CAMO volunteers do is merely a drop in the proverbial bucket of world poverty, it is important to remember that each "drop" is a life, a real live person, a Carmencita, a Manual, a Lydia, a Jose. A child, a mother, a father, a grandparent. A person whose life will now be better because of another person's kindness, another person's gift, another person's capacity to love.

CAMO was founded when the urge to cry was channeled into action.

On the edge of frustration.

In the face of despair.

And this is where the story really begins.

Where there is no vision, the people perish.[3]

The CAMO story is a journey, begun in 1979 when Kathryn Tschiegg, R.N. first traveled to Honduras to begin her life as a Peace Corps Volunteer at the Hospital de Occidente de Santa Rosa de Copán. For two years, Kathy worked alongside Honduran medical personnel in this small town high in the mountains, not far from the borders of Guatemala and El Salvador. This fair-haired woman from rural Orrville, Ohio, squarely in the American heartland, encountered a culture as foreign as she could imagine and a medical system – or lack thereof – that was unimaginable, a throw-back to Civil War era medicine in the United States.

It wasn't that the Hondurans didn't know what to do - that would have been merciful. Many of her counterparts had been U.S. trained or educated at the university in Tegucigalpa, the country's capital. No, the knowledge was there, but the tools were not.

Too often, Kathy recalls, there was nothing they could do but stand by helplessly and watch a patient die because this poor, poor hospital in this poor, poor country could not afford to buy the medicines, the equipment, the supplies, the tools needed to keep patients alive, much less ease suffering or prevent medical crises.

Kathy once told me that she knows exactly when CAMO was born in her mind. It was late in her two-year stint with Peace Corps, while carrying yet another infant to the morgue. She realized that, in that month alone, she had carried 31 dead infants to the morgue to be placed in rough-hewn wooden coffins. And why? Because no respirators were available to assist newborns with breathing, or no medicines existed to halt the debilitating diarrhea of cholera, or no antibiotics were available to combat life-threatening infections. It sorely challenged her faith in a merciful God, she told me. How could He allow this to happen? She felt she had to harden her heart to the misery around her or find some way to do something about it. The idea for CAMO struck, but it would be ten years before she could grow it beyond her own personal campaign to improve conditions there.

She shared her dream with her new-found friend, Honduran Gladys Castellanos, another young nurse at Hospital de Occidente.

It is important to note that this hospital in Santa Rosa was, until only recently, the only public hospital in that part of the country. It serves well over one-half million people throughout the five western 'states' of Honduras. Yet, this 202-bed hospital had not even the most basic medical equipment: no EKG machines, ventilators, ultrasounds, et cetera, et cetera, et cetera. Just about every doctor's office in the U.S. has an EKG. How is it possible, Kathy wondered, that a major hospital in Honduras has none?

CAMO has since changed that, thanks to the generosity of donors and volunteers here in the United States, and thanks to the foresight and determination of Kathy Tschiegg.

For Kathy, it began simply. She had returned to Ohio after her Peace Corps service and began working in a large city hospital. She found herself sickened by the waste in the American health care system: equipment discarded because something new had come on the market; medical implements mothballed because the doctor now prefers a different brand; sealed, sterile packaged supplies thrown away because national standards prohibit materials from going back into inventory once removed. Waste of perfectly usable tools, tools that her former patients in Honduras would die for...literally.

So, she began asking her colleagues to save the discarded, to let her know when new equipment was replacing out-dated, but working equipment. She enlisted a bio-engineer to assess and, if needed, repair the machines, so she could put them to use in Honduras. She visited her friend Gladys in Santa Rosa a couple of times over the next decade and brought many gifts - much needed medical equipment and supplies for the Hospital.

In 1992, Kathy enlisted five medical friends, doctors and nurses, to come along with her to do some basic training in surgery and general medicine. That first trip was so well received and appreciated by the Honduran medical personnel, that, within the year, she started investigating the possibility of incorporating as a 501(c)(3) charitable organization so she could expand the potential good of CAMO.

Central American Medical Outreach (CAMO) was incorporated as a non-profit charitable organization on May 17, 1993, but it was still operating as a fully volunteer organization. Kathy Tschiegg was also organizer and volunteer then. She still worked as a full-time nurse in the hospital and spent virtually all her free time collecting unused medical equipment and donated supplies, storing them in a nearby Amish barn until she could raise the money, through public speaking and personal requests, to ship it down. Gradually, she enlisted the help of more friends and the medical community, and the idea soon took on a life of its own. In 1996, the Board of Directors of CAMO agreed that it was time for the organization to move to the next level of development, and hired Kathy to work as a full-time paid executive director.

In 1997, 64 volunteers participated in working teams in Santa Rosa de Copán, La Majada and San Pedro Sula, as well as a number of scattered rural villages up to two hours away visited by the dental crew. CAMO has been recognized by the Honduran Minister of Health as a viable force in improving the quality of medical care and, hence, the quality of life in Honduras, and the requests for help are growing.

Thus far, the focus of CAMO efforts have been on the Hospital de Occidente de Santa Rosa de Copán in an effort to make it a quality regional hospital, with good equipment and knowledgeable staff. It is now a place where medical personnel from around Honduras can come for training and experience. CAMO has brought several Honduran doctors stateside to work in Ohio hospitals for two weeks at a time learning the equipment and procedures that will enable them to not only better perform back home but also to train their colleagues as well – and carry on quality medical care for generations to come.

In 1995, CAMO sponsored a young physical therapist from New Jersey – Nancy Hoge, P.T. – to spend a year (and eventually 18 months) in Santa Rosa de Copán to set up the first physical therapy department in a Honduran public hospital and to train a local nurse in basic physical therapy techniques. All of the equipment was donated to CAMO or purchased by CAMO through stateside donations. U.S. donors, too, financed the living expenses for Nancy, who volunteered that year of her life for this service and was paid no salary.

In 1996, CAMO installed in Santa Rosa the first mammography machine in a public medical facility and, in 1997, a second was requested and installed in San Pedro Sula. Training for the mammography technicians was held first in Santa Rosa, then CAMO instructors traveled to San Pedro Sula with the new trainees to work with them there to ensure that they understood and were operating the equipment and developing the films correctly. An American radiologist went along as well to oversee that work and found, once again, that his Honduran counterpart's knowledge was superb but that the tools just had not been there…until now.

Breast cancer. Infant mortality. Physical and occupational rehabilitation. Dental hygiene. The challenges of even the most economically advantaged societies are that much more magnified in a country too poor to acquire the tools of life.

I am not the first to question why any of us is placed on this Earth in such favorable economic, societal, familial, physical and spiritual circumstances as I and my CAMO friends from the U.S. Nor am I the first to question what responsibilities that places on those of us more fortunate than others. So I go where I am called and reflect on the words of the Lord: *For unto whomsoever much is given, of him shall be much required; and to whom men have committed much, of him they will ask the more.*[4]

Through CAMO, I have been able to witness volunteers and donors providing the tools and the teaching to bring new hope to the next generation in western Honduras. Life. Hope. Faith. Love. I have witnessed the generous sharing of these gifts, and it is good.

And I am the better for it.

Cari DeSantis

References

1. Matthew 25:29-40

2. John 20:29

3. Proverbs 29:18

4. Luke 12:48

Ye are the light of the world.

A city that is set on an hill cannot be hid.

Neither do men light a candle,
and put it under a bushel,
but on a candlestick;
and it giveth light unto all that are in the house.

Let your light so shine before men,
that they may see your good works,
and glorify your Father which is in heaven.

Matthew 7:20

Introduction

A few years back, as a private hospital executive, I was heavily involved in our national debate over the universal right to adequate medical care. In a country with unarguably the best health care system in the world, we asked, how could we let millions of Americans go without adequate health care? We argued that health care is a basic human right along with life, liberty and the pursuit of happiness. I still believe that, but I have since had my horizons broadened.

While we were arguing over who should get heart transplants and hip replacements, millions of our neighbors to the south went without any health care at all; children went deaf for the lack of antibiotics to treat simple ear infections; mothers died in childbirth because no ultrasound existed to guide physicians in diagnosing critical conditions; surgery was often riskier than the illness, with inappropriate anesthesia, unreliable electricity in the operating room, and no ventilators, monitors or other post operative assistive and diagnostic equipment to assure recovery.

In seven years as a hospital executive, I had seen all the medical miracles that money could buy. After five minutes in a public hospital in Honduras, I had seen the other side of the coin. It is amazing how one's perspective changes on a dirt path beneath banana trees under a dry, hot sun in the Central American mountains. Less than a day's travel from my home in Delaware, I was in a land where medical care was still being practiced much as it was when that trip would have taken a month or more, a hundred years ago. The Honduran doctors and nurses had the knowledge, but not the tools required to perform even the simplest procedures or the medicines to combat what we refer to as routine illnesses.

I was totally unprepared for the reality I faced on my first trip with Central American Medical Outreach – CAMO. Even my experience with the health care poor in this country was not enough to help me over the culture shock. We take so much for granted in the United States that when we venture outside our borders, we are often confronted with situations that are totally unimaginable to us. When is the last time you saw x-ray films drying on a tree in the hospital courtyard? Or surgical linens being sterilized in a boiling cauldron over an open wood fire then laid to dry and bleach on the ground in the sun outside?

I wanted to tell everyone I knew about these conditions, and I wanted to enlist my medical friends to help. So I took photographs. Lots of them.

The photographs in this book are but a few of the hundreds I shot over the three years I have been involved with Central American Medical Outreach. I started out capturing the unbelievable and found myself documenting progress. Over three years, the work of CAMO has made a difference. Much of that I have on film.

Through my camera lens, I saw so many touching moments: moments of joy and of sadness, of fear and of pain, of hope and of love. Photos of CAMO volunteers in action with patients and hospital staff; photos of the children in the orphanage run by the Missionaries of Charity of Calcutta and "adopted" by CAMO as a special project; photographs of the beautiful countryside in and around the western mountains of Honduras where I traveled to remote villages with dental teams bringing care where none had been before; and images of the wonderful, beautiful faces of the people I met along the way.

This book was born out of my desire to tell the CAMO story and to inspire others to join CAMO and similar humanitarian relief efforts in making this world a better place. But what photographs to choose? Which ones best told the story?

The photographs on the following pages are not necessarily "the best" artistically or technically; they were chosen because they illustrate the need and the hope. They are a tribute to the many Americans who volunteer all over the world and who daily renew my faith in humanity...and in a merciful God.

That's what this book is really all about – faith.

Faith in our personal commitments to service; faith in those who can show us the way; faith in a community of strangers dedicated to a common goal; faith in the inherent goodness of humankind; and faith in a loving God, whose plan we cannot know but who will guide us if we just listen...and look.

Cari DeSantis

"Preach the gospel daily.
Use words if necessary."

St. Francis of Assisi

Faith in Action

an essay by Mike Billington

It is in the desert, and perhaps only there, that a man can think clearly.

It is there that Jesus went, as did the prophets of Israel before him. And it is in those uncomplicated lands of sun and shadow where they came upon the great answers to the questions that beset us all.

For it is there, in those dried-out places, that the eye and the mind are least distracted. The browns and tans, the grays, blacks and reds of the desert do not compete for attention and, in so doing, crowd out thought.

The desert is a place for silent contemplation.

A place for reflection.

It is a place where, because there are no other distractions, God can truly be seen, not simply felt.

A place where faith can be discovered, tested, and made strong by the passage not only of time but of thought.

It is said often by well-meaning philosophers and by hucksters posing as preachers that we Americans live now in a spiritual desert; a wasteland devoid of faith and of hope, where charity is despised and goodness has been rendered obsolete.

It is not so.

You need only look around to see the lie of it.

For the simple truth is that there has been no other time in history when faith has been more alive.

Perhaps that's because we live today in an age of miracles. A time when, because of our technology and our affluence, even average men and women of faith can do more than simply contemplate the meaning of God's will. It is only now that not only the rich and powerful but also the laborer can readily translate faith into action.

And so they are going forth into neighborhoods, and into foreign lands, to share what they have with those who have not.

It is such people who make up the heart, and the literal soul, of Central American Medical Outreach. There are certainly rich men and women among CAMO's volunteers who go yearly to work to the rugged highlands of western Honduras, but the majority of these who invest their time and money in service to the poorest of the poor are not counted in their number.

We live in an age where there is no faith?

Where hope is dead?

Those who have profited from spreading that libel – and those who, unfortunately, believe it – have not seen CAMO's volunteer doctors and nurses working into the night to repair shattered bodies and make them whole again.

They have not seen CAMO volunteers patiently teaching, working with the poor, and finding solutions to problems that had once appeared all but insoluble.

They have not ridden for hours in the back of pick-up trucks to remote mountain villages with volunteer CAMO dentists who spend their vacations among the poor instead of on the golf course.

Nor will they. It is a sad truth that bad news sells better than good news. The naysayers have always known that, and they have always made a comfortable living spreading the bad news to those gullible enough to discount the evidence before them in favor of rumor and innuendo.

And so it is that the volunteers who toil in the heat and humidity of western Honduras do not get into the newspapers very often. Nor are they featured on the nightly news.

They are not troubled by that, for they do not go for glory.

They go to serve.

To exercise their faith.

And to share what they have with those who have not.

In the case of CAMO's volunteers, what they are sharing is quite literally the gift of life in a region where even minor illnesses can mean death and where an injury, that would be only inconvenient in an America that has taken health care for granted, can often rob a man of his ability to work forever.

The author John Steinbeck once reflected that, as a natural consequence of their births, all humans are caught in a perpetual net of good and evil.

Virtue and vice, he said, were at war in the human heart when man first set foot on the earth and they will be there when the last human breathes his last breath.

And so it is, Steinbeck said, that when a man comes near to the end of his time on earth, he has only one hard, clean question to ask of his life.

"Was it good or evil? Have I done well – or ill?"

The many people of good will, who have put their faith into action by performing selfless service to people they do not know and may never meet again without hope of reward or profit, can answer that question without equivocation.

"Yes," they can say, "it was good."

The Photographs

What secrets lie within this heart?

Abandoned by a family that cannot spare the time to care for him

Malnourished.

He lives in the orphanage in Santa Rose de Copán and spends his waking hours in this chair.

His eyes are focused on a point far away; a point that only he can see.

What secrets lie within his heart?

What dreams does he dream when he sleeps?

What might he become?

Is he the one who will one day find the cure for cancer? The one who will write the novel that will influence a generation? Will he become the father of a fine young son? The hard-working husband of a hard-working woman?

Not without help. Not without food for his body and nourishment for his soul.

Could you be the one who has the key; the one that will unlock the secrets that lie within his heart?

Santos

Two by Two...

They lay head to foot, their babies gathered close to their bodies.

There is not enough space in the maternity ward at the Hospital de Occidente; not even for a mother to spend those first few precious hours of her baby's life alone with her child.

The hospital serves the needs of 600,000 people spread across five western states in Honduras. It squats atop a small rise in the hilly city of Santa Rosa de Copán. Its walls are thick and in need of paint. Each ward, even this ward, is open to the air.

Many women have to travel for a day or more to get to this crowded hospital so they can have their babies under a doctor's care. It is an arduous journey on crowded, noisy buses that leak exhaust. Undeterred, the mothers come for the sake of their children. They know the journey will not be easy. They know the hospital will be crowded. They know they will probably have to share a bed with another mother when they arrive. Yet, still, they come.

They have little choice. There are few doctors in the countryside. There are few clinics. If their babies are going to have the best chance to live past their first birthday, the women must make the journey. They must share a bed with someone they do not know. They must lie awake if the other mother's baby cannot sleep.

And yet that is little enough to pay for a chance to have your baby born under a doctor's care. It is a small-enough sacrifice when the alternative is weighed out: A birth in a small house, attended by no one but a neighbor whose only real qualification may be that she gave birth and survived the experience, even if her baby did not.

In Honduras, as many as four in 10 babies die before they celebrate a year of life. The women who come to the Hospital de Occidente have likely never seen that statistic.

But they know it. They know in their hearts that a baby born outside the hospital has less of a chance to live than one born inside. They have stood helplessly by as the infant sons and daughters of their neighbors, their cousins, and their sisters surrendered their spirits.

And so they come to the Hospital de Occidente

Where they lie head to foot, two in a bed with their newborn babies gathered close by their bodies.

Two by Two

Old man, alone...

No one came to visit him on Tuesday as he lay in his bed.

No one but the nurses, who checked regularly to make sure that the IV bag jury-rigged to a couple of 2X2's was still drip-drip-dripping nourishment into his thin body.

No one but the doctor as he made his rounds, pausing briefly to read the hand-drawn number on the end of his bed, matching it with the hand-drawn chart.

He lived too far away for his family to make the trip, for they owned no car and buses cost money that was needed elsewhere. Visiting him would have meant the loss, too, of a day's labor.

And so he lay there alone, his eyes closed, his breathing shallow but regular. His heart beating with the steady rhythm of a man much stronger than he looked.

Was there a time when he reached his strong arms down to pick up his child? Was there a time when those arms wrapped themselves around his wife's waist?

Perhaps there was a day when his heart beat faster as he struggled to carry a heavy load through the heat, breathing deeply of the thin mountain air. Perhaps there was a time when his heart beat faster as he watched his son drawing near to him after a long absence.

Are these the memories that passed through his mind on that Tuesday as he lay alone in his bed, his thin body nourished only by the drip-drip-dripping bag that was attached to thin pieces of wood nailed together to form a makeshift IV pole?

No one knows.

For no one came to visit him.

Except the doctor.

And the nurse.

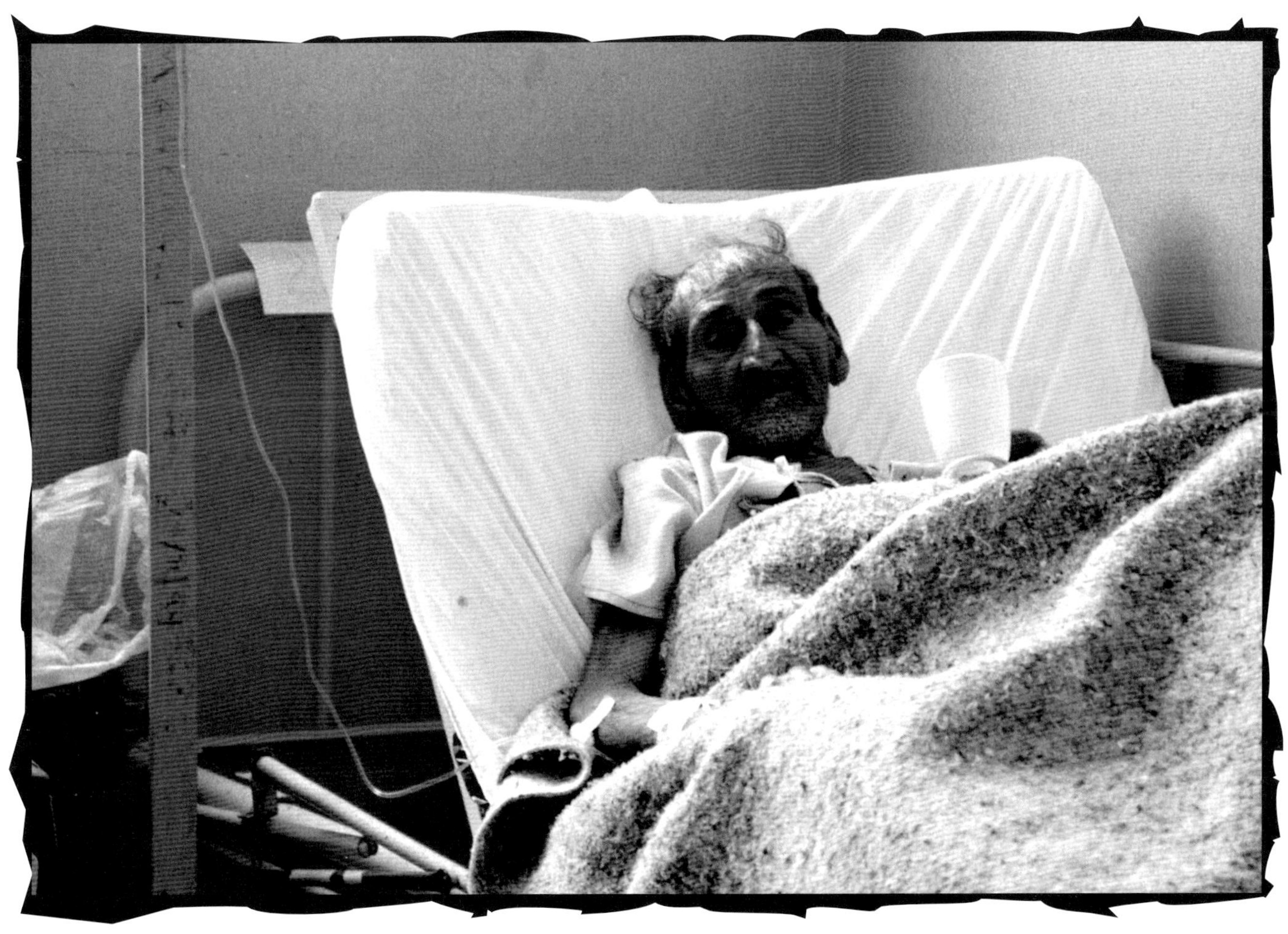

Viejo

The open door…

"Death hath so many doors to let out life"
John Fletcher

Who is it that shall stand guard at Death's door?

Who is it that shall stand there, stolidly, to hold back those cold winds as they try to enter?

Who is it that will trust in the Lord even when all seems hopeless?

Who will not flinch when the time draws near for the final conflict between life and death even though all the hordes of hell cry for this child?

This man?

This woman?

Who will have the courage to stand there in the doorway, forbidding entrance to those dark collectors who come to take the life of this child?

This man?

This woman?

Is it you who has that faith? You who can lay claim to that particular brand of courage? Is it you who will be there when Death comes knocking?

There is a time to be born, a time to grow.

A time to weep, a time to sow.

There is a time to live.

And a time to die.

Who will stand in the doorway when an impatient Death comes early?

I will, Lord.

With your help, I can.

And I will.

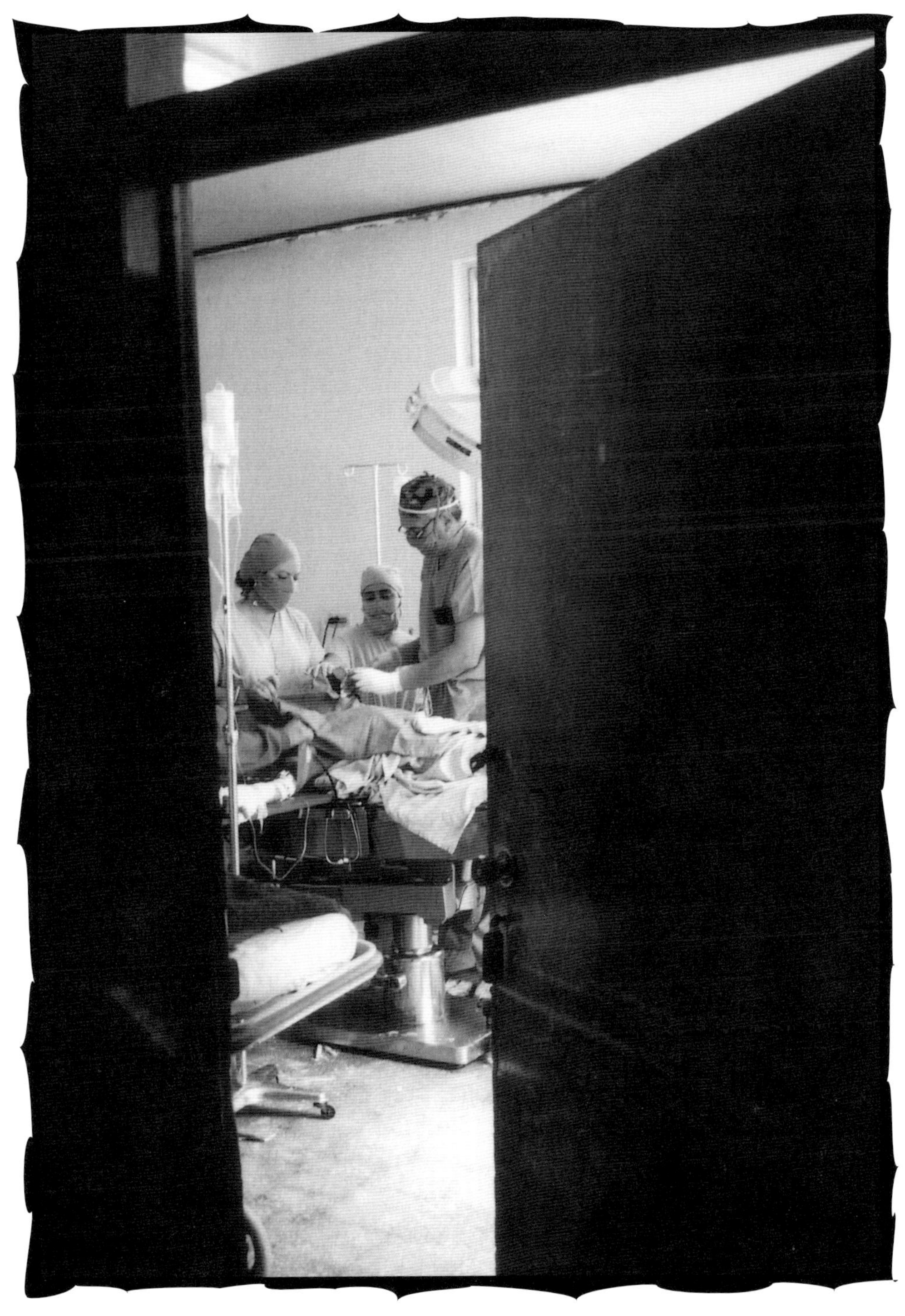

Death's Door

Mírna...

In Santa Rosa de Copán the nurses do not have the equipment at their fingertips that nurses have come to rely upon in the United States.

And so they make do with the tools they have at hand:

Compassion.

Perseverance.

Commitment.

Caring.

Hope.

Faith.

Above all, faith.

Mirna

The morgue...

Death does not cast his baleful eye
on the Hospital de Occidente
from some proud tower. No.
Here he sits in a small building,
separate from the others, and waits.
Not for long. Never for very long.
In one month, 31 tiny caskets were carried
to his door and gently placed
inside the darkness to wait for the angels
to carry them home.
And even Death wept for them.

When Angels Weep

Pediatrics ward...

There are cribs on the pediatrics ward now.

There were none before.

But there are still no sheets

for my child to lie down upon in the darkness

when the nights are cold

and the chill air reaches

up from the floor to caress his small body.

There is so much more

this hospital still needs

but at least we are not sleeping on the floor.

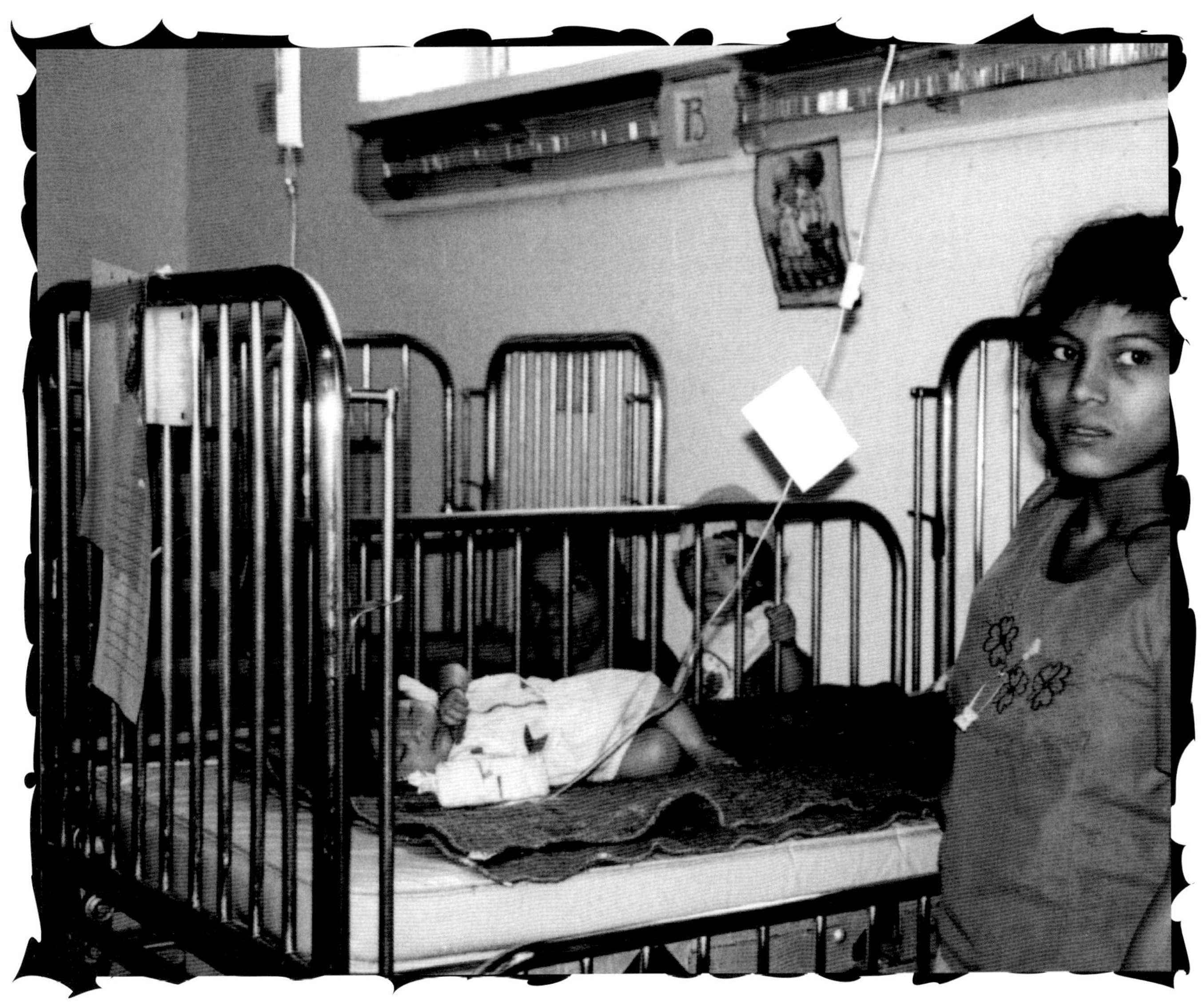

Tender Mercies

The orphan...

He was orphaned by design,
left with the Sisters
by parents for reasons that
they, only they, know.
He knew them for two short months
before they took him
to the orphanage at night
and walked away
into the gloom
leaving behind no
trace of their love; no address
for his dreams, his hopes.
Life can be a test of strength,
and sometimes living
takes more courage than dying.

Orphan – Hogar de San José
Santa Rosa de Copán, Honduras, C.A.

Women's medical ward...

They bring their own blankets when they come to the hospital.

Too poor to afford nightgowns, they often sleep in their own clothes.

Their IV's are hung on 2X2's. Their charts crudely drawn by nurses.

Women do not come to the hospital on a whim.

Many are near death when they finally make the trip for they know when they go there is no one else to care for their families while they are gone. Their husbands must work if the family is to eat and cannot afford to stay home to watch those children who are, themselves, too young to work.

They know, too, that they must pay $3 a day to be in the hospital. To a Honduran mountain family, that is a major expense especially since the lack of antibiotics and equipment often means they will remain in the hospital for weeks at a time.

So they wait until they must go.

Or die.

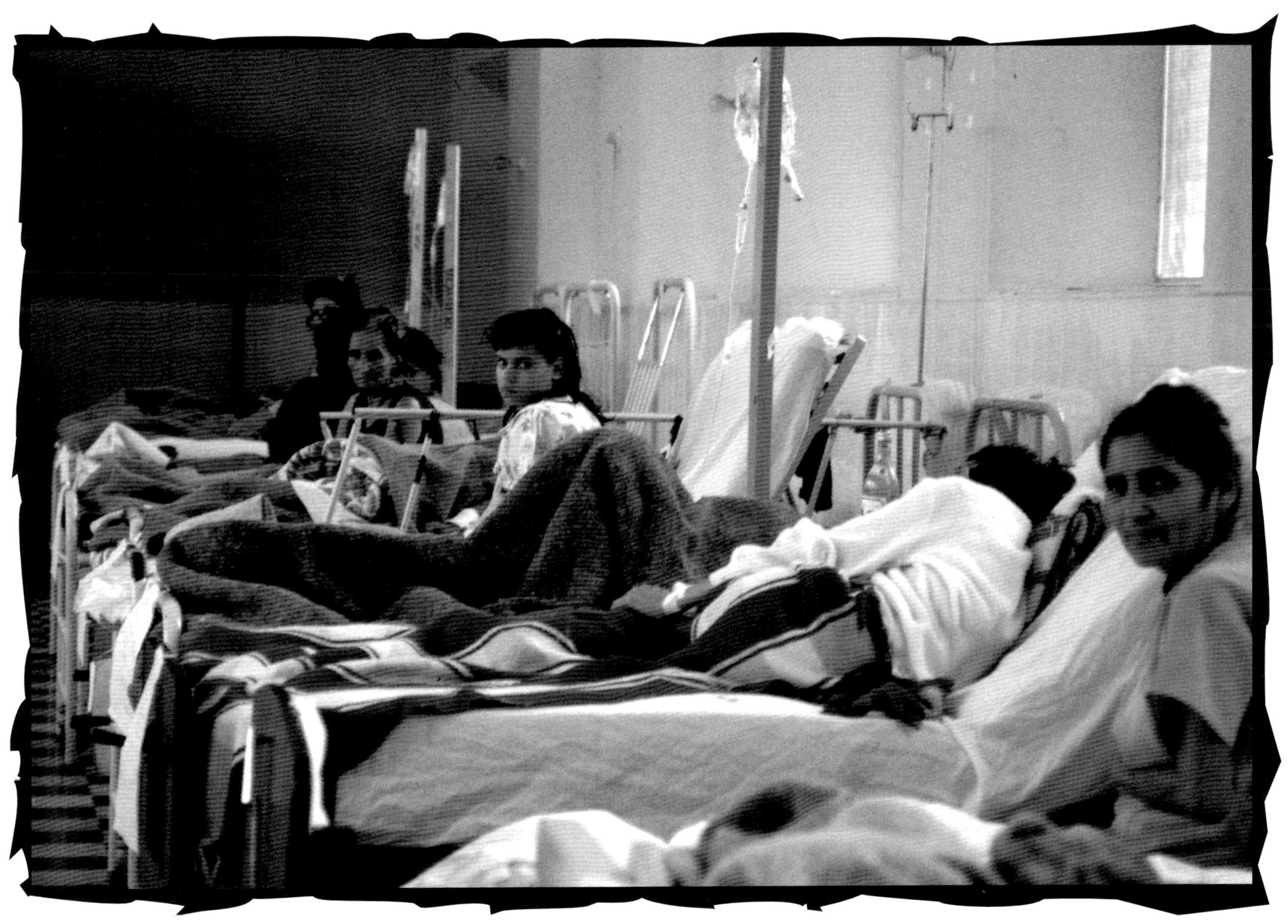

Women's Ward

The sister...

Silver and gold have I none; but such as I have give I thee.

I give what I have away.

For, having nothing, I yet possess all things.

Hermana de La Esperanza

A mother's love...

There are not enough nurses to go around.

So I stay by his side.

Bathing him.

Washing his clothes.

By hand.

I have learned, in the year I have been here by his side, to care for him.

His father comes to visit when he can.

It is hard for him. This is our son who was so strong. Who could work all day.

Now he cannot breathe without a tube in his throat.

When his father goes back home, I stay.

As I will.

Until he goes home.

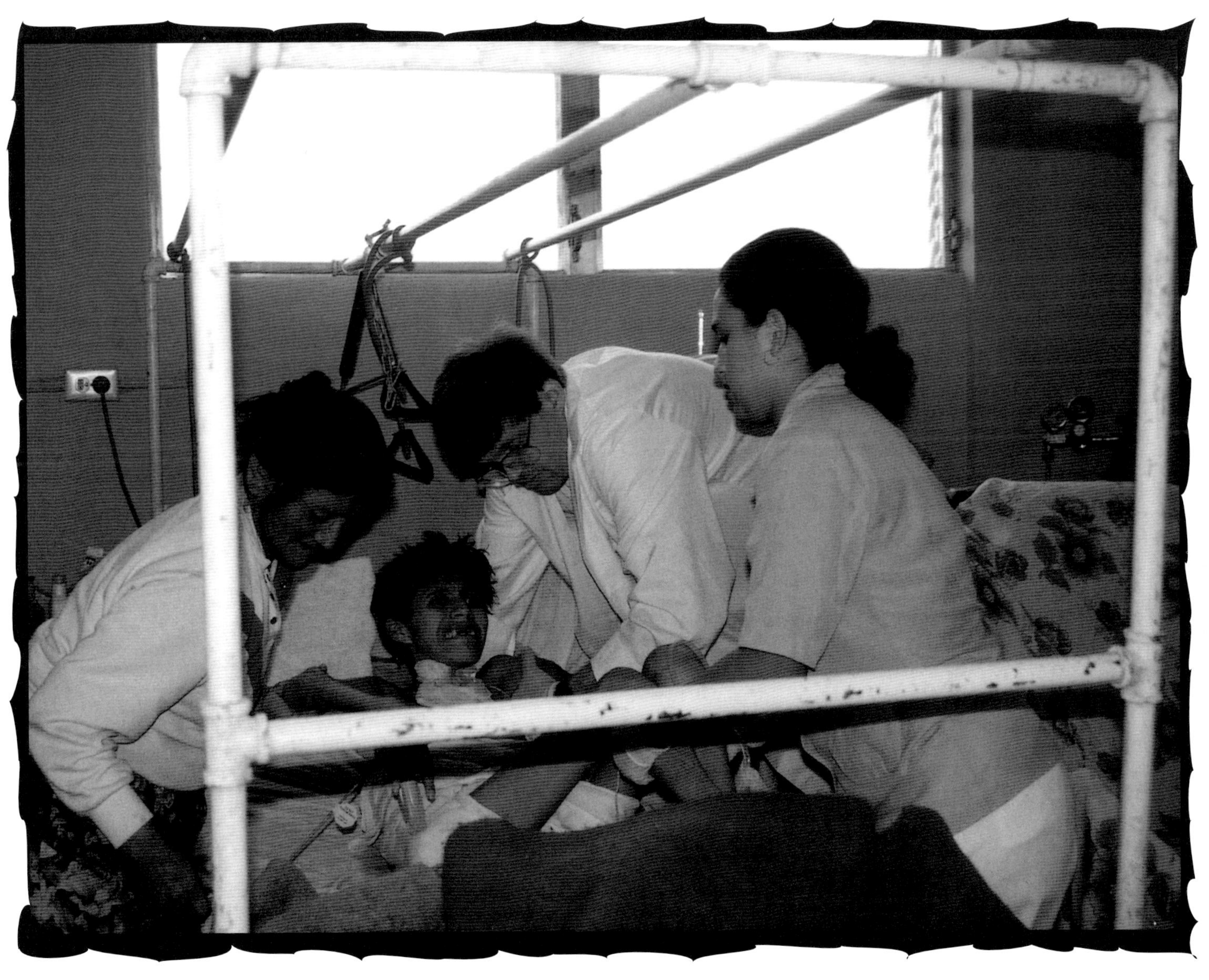

Amor de Madre

Vulture...

The vulture, big and black,
drifted through the still air,
stretched out its claws
and settled lightly
onto the hospital chapel's cross.
It spread its midnight wings wide
then tucked them in close
to its glossy body.
The gringos were alarmed.
Don't be, the old ones said.
The bird is a good omen, they said.
Many people will be healed today,
they said, and crossed themselves.
God has turned his face toward us
and He is smiling.

A Good Day for Surgery

Give me strength...

Lord, the days are long and they are so often filled with frustration.

There are so many patients.

And they are so sick.

We do not have the equipment to care for them properly. We do not have the medicines. We do not always have the skill to make them well.

Give me the strength I need to care for the sick who come to my door.

Give me the skill to make them well again.

Give me the strength to work even when I am tired.

Give me the courage to continue even when I fail.

Give me the strength, Lord, to do your bidding.

Let my faith be strong enough to be the instrument of Your will.

Dame Fortaleza – Dr. Ricardo Dominguez

Be not afraid...

The dentist had just pulled one of her baby teeth and she could taste blood in her mouth.

It frightened her; enough that she almost cried. It took a tremendous effort for her to hold back the tears; to steel her body and her resolve not to act like a baby and embarrass both herself and her family.

It did not hurt, she told the volunteer who came to comfort her. But the needles and the probes and the pliers were frightening to see.

And the dentist was so big... so strong.

Her brown eyes were grown large with fright. Her heart was beating fast, thumping in her chest.

"Hold my hand. Squeeze it tightly. Don't be afraid. It's all over now," the volunteer said when she sat down next to the little girl.

I am with you.

La Niña Loses a Tooth

Sisters...

They come from different worlds.

They shared nothing until they enlisted as foot soldiers in the daily struggle to save people's lives.

And yet they are sisters.

Their faith has made them part of the same family. It is a faith as strong as a blood bond; stronger, perhaps, than those ties that come undone in so many families when crisis strikes.

Their sisterhood was forged in long hours working among the poorest of the poor. They have spent their days caring for those no one else would care for; they have spent their nights comforting those who had no one else to comfort them.

They have prayed for the souls of people whose names they did not know.

They have shed tears for those whose lives they could not save.

For those whose wounds they could not bind up.

For those whose illnesses were stronger than the medicines they had at hand.

And when the crying was done they went back to the struggle, the never-ending struggle that is their life's work.

Their calling.

Together, they have borne many burdens.

So many burdens.

And, together, they have wrought miracles.

So many miracles.

Hermanas del Alma –
Kathryn Tschiegg y Gladys Castellanos,
Santa Rosa de Copán, Honduras, C.A.

I heard the voice of the Lord, saying,
Whom shall I send and who will go for us?
Then said I, Here am I; send me.

Isaiah 6:8

The touch...

He heard the volunteers had come back to Santa Rosa de Copán once again.

Bringing their medicines with them.

And their power to heal the sick.

So her father brought her to the Hospital de Occidente.

She tried to be brave but she was nervous.

The volunteers were big; bigger than her Papa.

And they seemed to know magic.

They have the power to hear your heart beating.

They can look into your eyes, it is said, and tell if you are well.

People such as these could do great harm if they are not kind, she thought.

But then the big man with the kind eyes knelt down next to her.

And reached out with his big hands and touched her gently on the shoulder.

And smiled.

He spoke to her in Spanish.

Telling her it would be all right.

Telling her that the stethoscope was not magic.

Only a tool, like a spoon or a hoe.

The girl smiled back.

A simple touch.

Wonderful medicine.

The Right Touch

Carlos...

The doctor had flown more than a thousand miles and survived a three-hour ride along roads not known for their quality to get to the Hospital de Occidente in Santa Rosa de Copán.

And when they brought him this tiny baby, who was literally wasting away because of an obstruction that did not allow him to process food, he gathered several Honduran doctors and nurses around him and, together, they performed the surgery that they hoped would save his life. The other doctors and the nurses learned a great deal that morning.

Later, after the operation, the doctor went to check on his young patient.

All the vital signs were good.

So good that two hours later, the little boy was removed from the only working isolette the hospital had so that another, sicker, child could be placed inside it.

Thirty minutes later, the boy was dead.

It is said that a carpenter can blame his tools when a job doesn't turn out right.

But what if there are no tools?

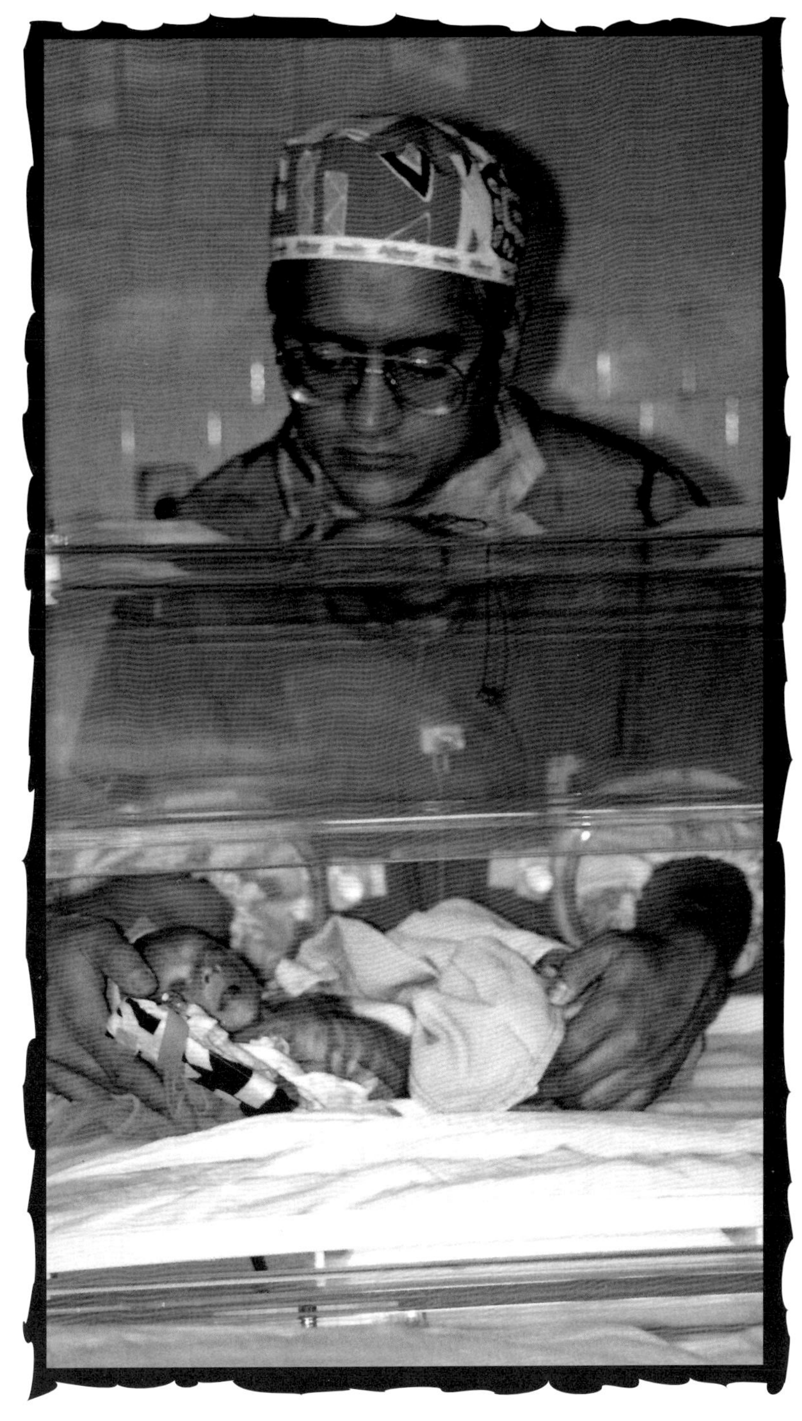

Dr. Carlos Duran, Neonatologist

The churchkeeper...

She has been caring for the church for a very long time.

Every day, she sweeps the aisles, dusts the statues, and has a kind word for those who come bringing their petitions to God.

She has seen so many come seeking refuge; seeking a respite from the storms that have swept over their lives.

And she has seen the volunteers come.

They bring medicine and machines when they come.

They bring smiles.

They bring hugs, and warmth, laughter, and faith.

And hope.

Most of all, hope.

The Churchkeeper & The Doctor

The doctor…

Back home, there are orderlies to wheel the patients into and out of surgery.

Back home, his operating room is full of modern equipment and a platoon of highly-trained nurses. The power never fails back home. The temperature is controlled.

Back home, his patients schedule their appointments. They don't just show up asking if there will be time for them this year.

In Santa Rosa de Copán, there are no orderlies, so the volunteer doctor often brings his patients back to the wards.

He doesn't seem to mind.

And he doesn't seem to mind the string of 14 and 15-hour days he works in an operating room that has an air-conditioner sticking its rusted snout through the window.

And if the Honduran nurses don't have the same level of training as his stateside nurses do, he looks upon that as an opportunity to do some teaching, sharing the knowledge he has with people who can put it to such very good use once he leaves.

After all, that's what it is all about.

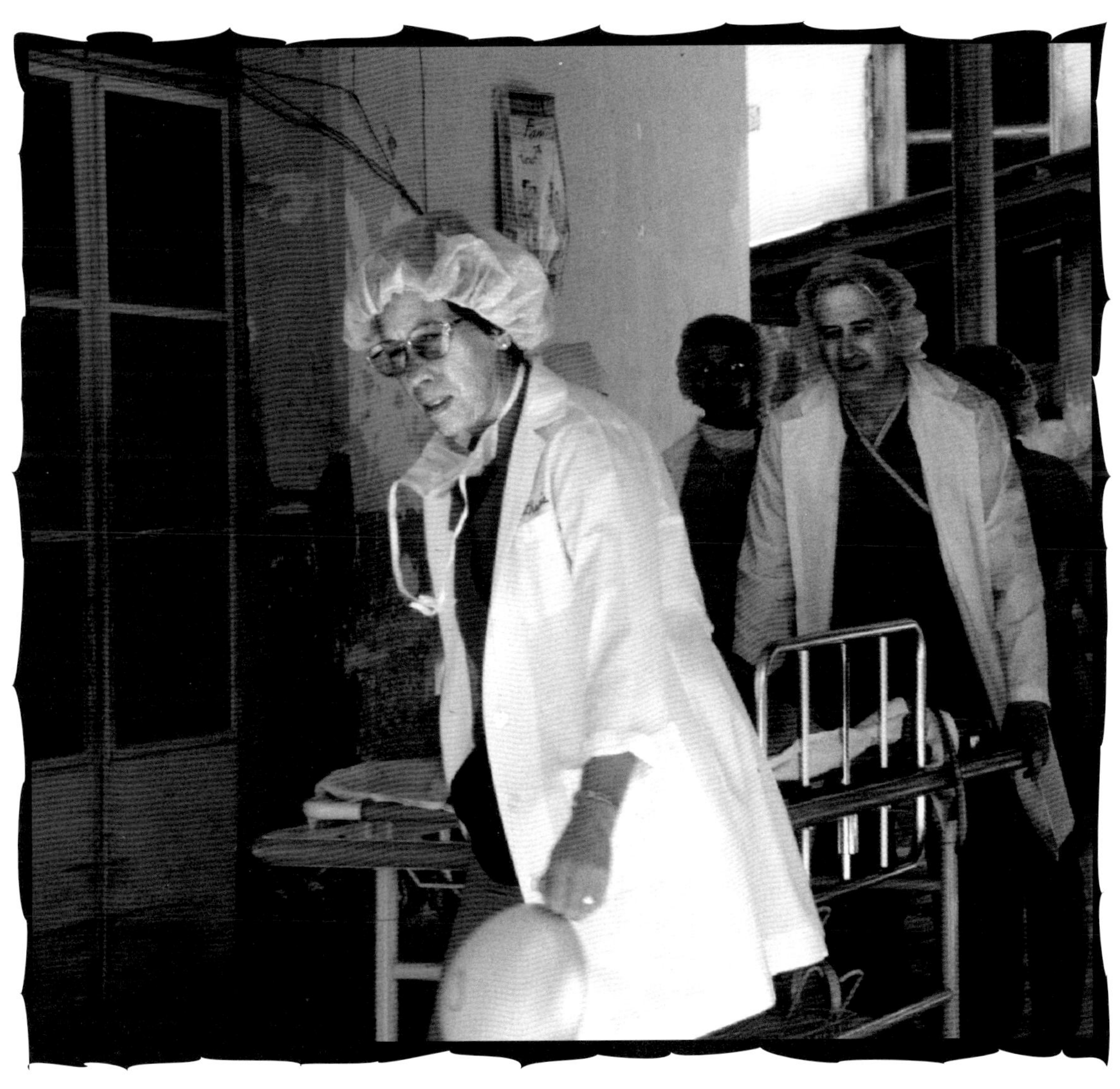

Post-surgical Transport
Santa Rosa de Copán

Two mothers...

One is a volunteer, a mother herself.

Back home in Delaware, she teaches mothers how to care for their new babies.

At the Hospital de Occidente she spent her vacation doing the same.

The other had just given birth to her first child.

She brought a threadbare towel from home to wrap the baby in.

And shared a bed with another woman and her new baby.

The volunteer and the new mother had almost nothing in common.

Except their motherhood.

It was enough.

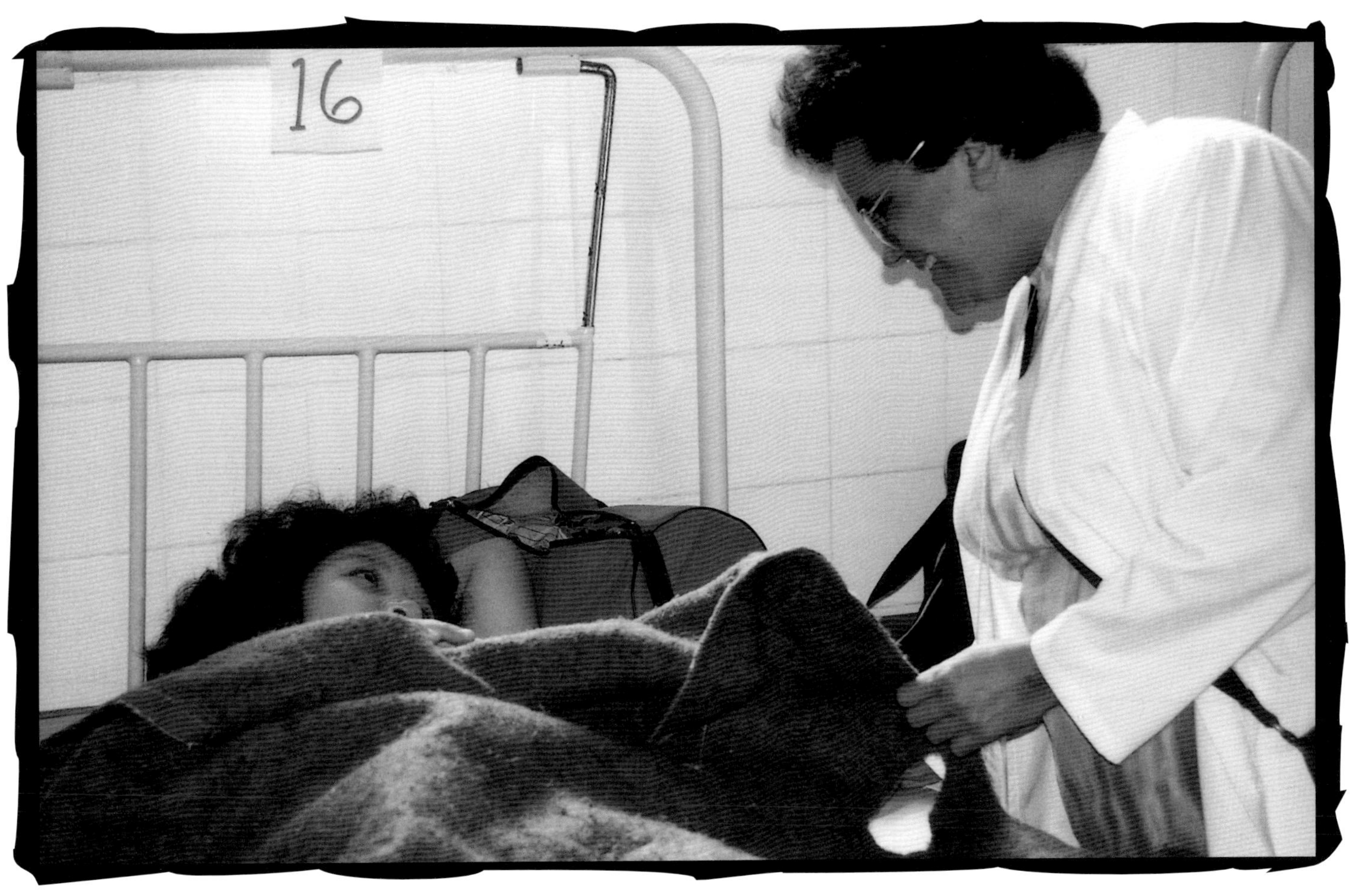

A Common Bond

Ojos Lindos...

I have heard of thee by the hearing of the ear;
but now mine eye seeth thee.
Proverbs 42:5

Though her life has been short,

her eyes have seen much.

They have seen women cry

for losing a child.

They have seen men fight back

the falling of tears.

And yet these eyes of hers,

these beautiful eyes,

have lost none of their hope.

They mirror her belief

that these people

she has heard so much about

will banish the pain

and make her well.

Ojos Lindos

A step at a time...

When CAMO installed a donated mammography machine in the Hospital de Occidente, it marked the first time that poor women could benefit from this technology. No other public hospital in the country had a mammography machine at that time and women still have to travel long distances to go there for check-ups.

At first, the doctors at the hospital encountered some resistance from an unexpected quarter. Many of their colleagues counseled their female patients not to have a mammogram. The reason: They had heard that mammography was not safe. That it might, in fact, cause a woman to develop the same breast cancer it was supposed to detect.

Still, the women came. Against the advice of their doctors. They came despite strong social taboos about baring their bodies to strangers.

The doctors at the Hospital de Occidente, however, soon discovered that knowing someone has cancer and treating it are two different things. In some cases, the women they diagnosed with cancer required surgery that the doctors had not enough time to perform. They needed chemotherapy that the doctors could not provide.

It is frustrating for the doctors to know exactly what to do and yet be unable to do it. They are ready now to take the next step. CAMO is there to walk beside them.

And so the journey continues.

A step at a time.

The First Mammogram

Santa Rosa de Copán, Honduras, C.A.

Mother, father and son...

Mother, father and son rode half a day in a cramped pick-up truck

along dusty roads to a small village in the mountains.

Dentists, the father and the son

would spend the late morning and most of the afternoon

tending to the teeth of the children there, while

the woman, who was both wife and mother,

tended to the children's emotional needs.

They cleaned teeth, pulled teeth, and filled cavities.

She handed out hugs and kind words to all who needed them.

Service. It is a family affair.

El Padre y el Hijo

Really Mom...

The glasses will help her see better.

They will enable her to do better in school.

Deep down, she knows that. Closer to the surface, however, she knows with the certainty that children know everything there is to know, that her friends are going to giggle when they see her wearing them.

One final plea: Mama, do I have to wear these things?

Yes.

You must.

And you will be grateful.

There are few eye doctors in the mountains of western Honduras, but even if there were more, not many people can afford to see them for regular examinations. The money that would be spent on eye doctors and glasses can be put to many other uses. Like food.

The results are not hard to see: Children who struggle to learn to read because they cannot see the page in front of them clearly, or cannot see the blackboard at all. Women whose useful lives are shortened because they can no longer thread a needle. Men who cannot see well enough to work at their trades.

But all of that is meaningless to a young lady who would rather look like a movie star than a librarian.

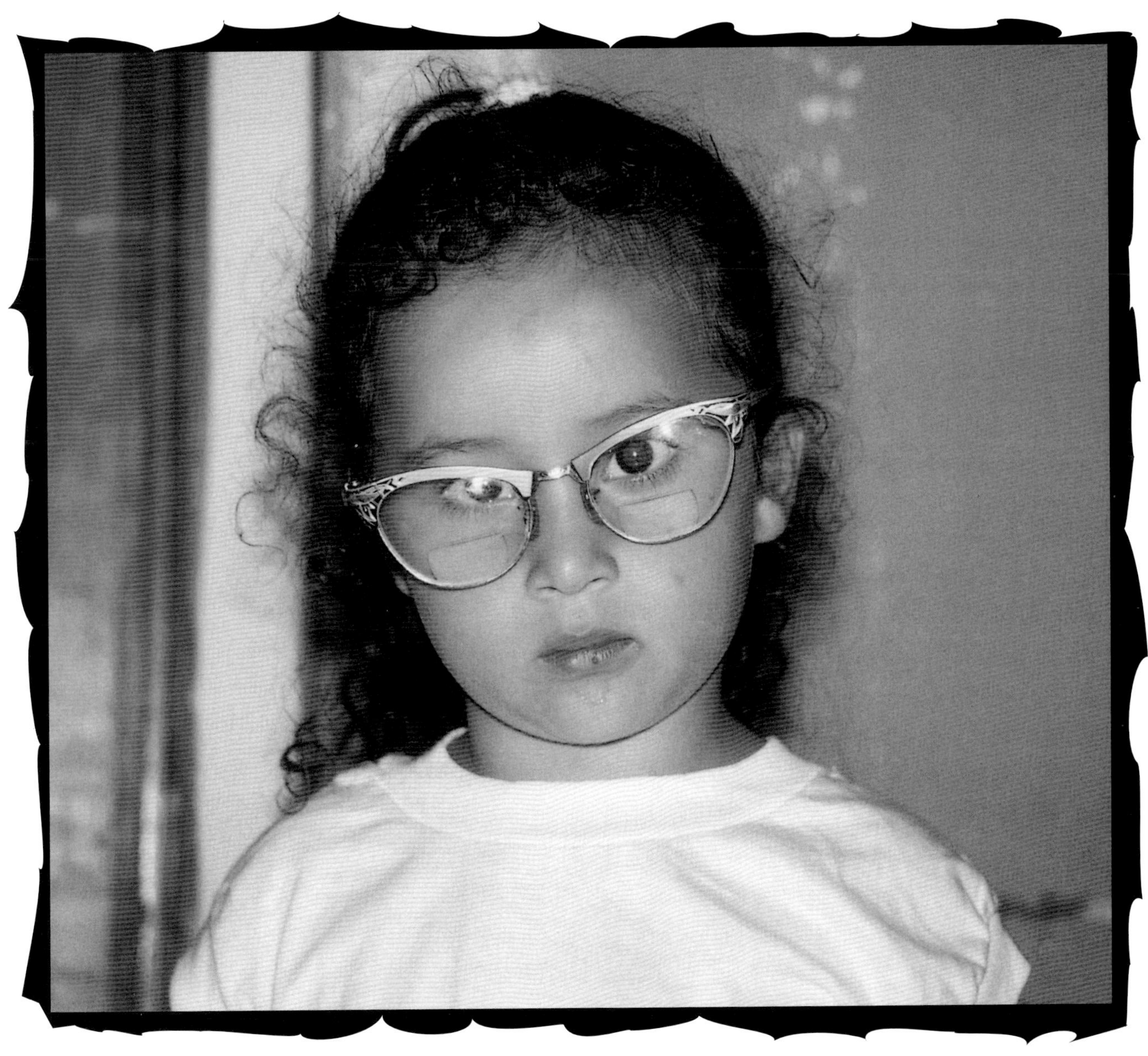

How Will She See The World Now?

A passport...

It looks like a simple collection of metal tubes.

But donated walkers and canes are so much more than that to these older men and women whose legs can no longer carry them the way they once did.

For men and women who would otherwise have remained seated for the rest of their lives, a walker or a cane is a passport.

A ticket to freedom.

It gives them access to the rest of the old-age home they live in.

Access to each other.

And access to the rest of the world.

El Pasaporte

Danilo…

He was born a child of sorrow.

Abandoned by his parents.

He could not sit up on his own, could not talk.

He was limp, nearly lifeless, when he was left

at the Hospital de Occidente.

At five years old, he weighed the same as a two-year-old.

The nurses and the doctors kept him alive.

Without much hope.

They could do no more.

Physical therapist Nancy Hoge could.

She saw something deep in his eyes.

A spark. A life.

Within six months she had him walking, eating and talking.

God had a plan.

A family in Pennsylvania, with much love to give,

took this child born in sorrow

into their home and a new life full of hope.

Danilo

The eye doctor...

There are two ways to help people see.

One is with prescriptions and glasses.

In a small room in the Hospital's surgical wing, the CAMO eye team has been bringing the gift of sight to thousands of men, women, and children for the past several years. Using donated equipment and donated glasses, the doctors, nurses, and volunteers have patiently checked the eyesight of anyone willing to wait in line for a chance to once again see the world clearly. The hours are long and the room is dark and often overheated because of the black vinyl covering the windows and the number of patients crowded inside its four walls.

The other way to help people see is more subtle.

It is through actions, by living your faith.

The eye team works all year collecting glasses for the people of western Honduras. When they travel to Santa Rosa they are unfailingly polite and patient. They greet everyone with a smile. They soothe ruffled nerves, calm fearful children, and, in so doing, they help people see in another way entirely.

They help the people, who have often walked miles hoping the doctors can help them, see that their faith was justified, because the living faith of the volunteers is just as strong.

The eye team helps the people who come for glasses see that compassion is not dead.

There is hope for a brighter world.

Dr. Ron Helps Them See

The helper...

One so big,

one so small

doing what they can

to live God's plan

in the hospital high

in the mountains

where even the sick

lend a hand.

El Ayudante

A hand to hold...

When I was frightened,

though you did not know me,

you were there

to hold my hand

and calm my fears

with soothing words

and I was no longer afraid.

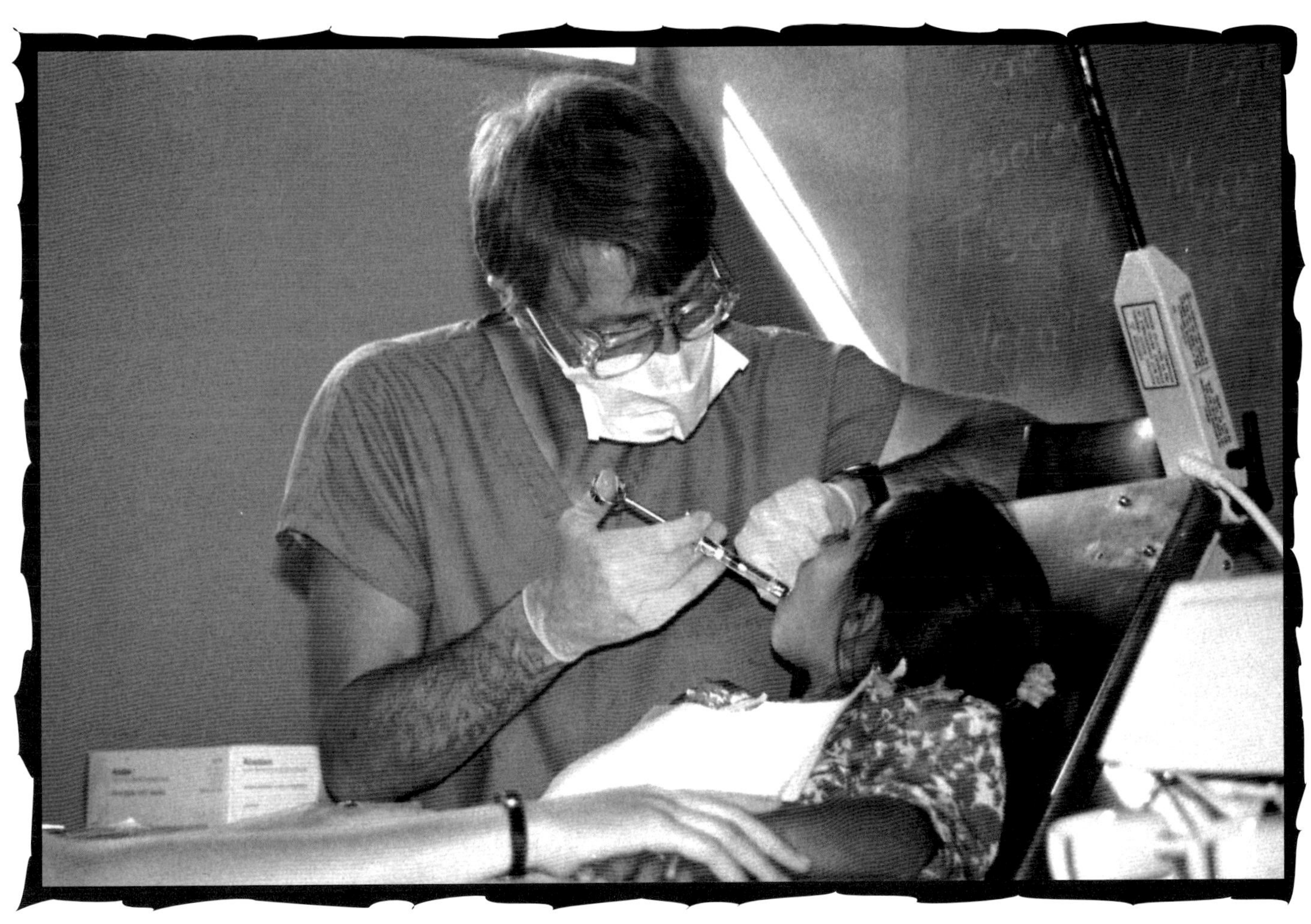

Un gesto de consuelo

The meal...

It is good food,
and not fine words,
that keeps me alive.

Moliere

The Bread of Life

Changing lives…

It is not only the people of Santa Rosa de Copán whose lives are changed when the volunteers arrive.

Each man and woman who has made the journey, who has spent endless hours tending to the sick, jury-rigging equipment so the doctors and nurses can use it to save lives, teaching the staff new techniques, or simply holding hands with scared children returns changed by that experience.

For some, the change is radical. A Peace Corps volunteer who served as a translator for CAMO one winter was so inspired by what he saw that he went to medical school.

For many, however, the change is a gentle one — a renewed sense of faith, a deeper understanding of the healing power of God's love, a better understanding of the common bond that unites us all, wherever we are.

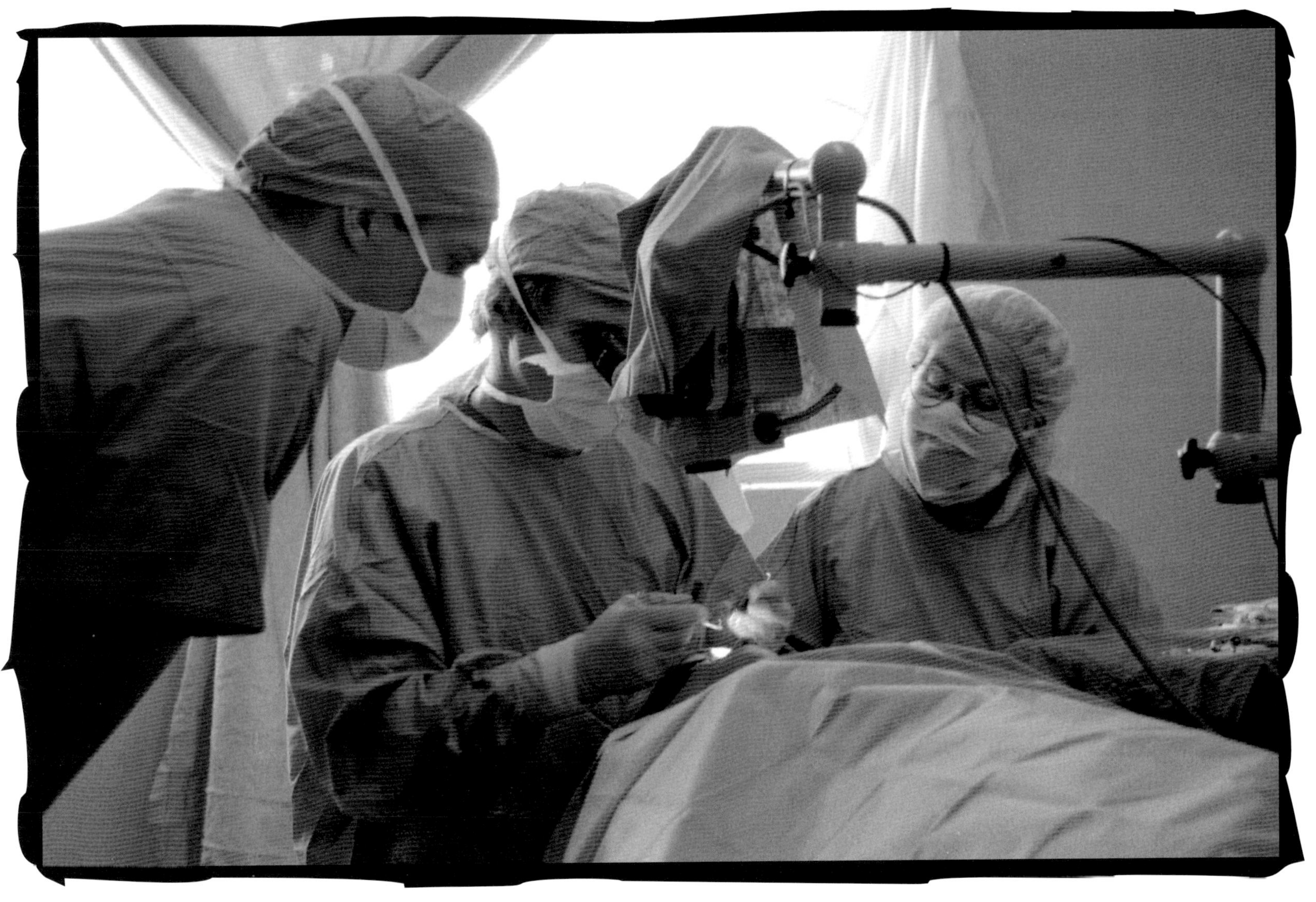

Destiny

Sonrisa

"Whatsoever a man soweth, that shall he also reap,"
Paul wrote to the Galations.

It is within our power, then, to sow good or ill, and so why should we not sow good wherever we go?

Why should we not perform a simple act of kindness to bring a smile to an old woman's face?

To her heart?

In Santa Rosa de Copán, there are many old men and women who are in need of the smiles that something as simple as a few minutes of pleasant conversation can bring. After a lifetime of toil, of being busy, there is perhaps no greater loss than the sense of purpose that work — no matter how hard and arduous — can bring.

People need to be included in life. They need new experiences, the kind that a visitor from a land they have only heard about can bring to them. They need the sense that they are valued. They need to feel that life would be poorer without them.

Is this medicine? This stopping by to visit with those who have lived so long?

Yes. As surely as handing out pills and performing operations, this is medicine.

With a bonus.

For as you sow, so shall ye reap... if you can bring a smile to someone, you will get one in return.

No pill can promise as much.

Smile!

By the skill of their hands...

The patients seldom, if ever, see them;
the volunteers who work behind the scenes
in the hospital, repairing broken equipment,
checking valves and gauges, making certain that
when the doctor flips a switch or turns a knob
everything happens just as it should.
We all have special gifts;
talents that make miracles possible.

...De Sus Manos

The boy with no ears...

He was born without ears

and so everyone assumed he could not hear.

But they were wrong.

The gringos discovered he could indeed hear,

though not well.

With prosthetic ears,

and a hearing aid,

they gave him a life

full of the joyous noise of his family

and a chance to live as others do.

Silence Broken

A true operating theater…

The arrival of medical and dental volunteers from the United States is often a social event in the tiny villages of the Honduran highlands.

There are not many gringos, after all, who are willing to make the long, dusty, bumpy trips to these small places, some of which have been there for three and four centuries.

So it was when a CAMO dental team visited Oramilaca. People from throughout the village, and from scattered homes nearby, came to see the dentist at work. They watched him check teeth and gums, pull some teeth, fill others.

And when it was done, and the dentist had gone back to Santa Rosa de Copán, they gathered to talk about what they had seen. To discuss, in somber tones, the meaning of the visit - why they were so blessed - and the possibility that the dental team would come back the next year.

Truly, it was a day to be remembered.

The Operating Theatre
Oramilaca, Honduras, C.A.

Joy...

They flew, like fairies in some old tale, on the little breezes that crept over the orphanage wall and floated up and down as the children stood, at first, with their mouths wide open and their eyes staring.

They had never, in their short lives so filled with hunger and abandonment, seen such a wondrous thing as a soap bubble.

The CAMO volunteers were a little taken aback when, suddenly, the children's thin voices broke into laughter so joyous that it seemed almost unreal.

Could something so simple as soap bubbles floating in the air, something that is taken for granted by every child in America, be that wonderful?

Yes.

But it was not only the dancing bubbles, with their tiny rainbows dancing along the curve of their bodies, that made the children laugh so joyously.

It was the fact that someone had cared enough to add something to their lives, something strange and yet not terrifying. The children in the orphanage at Santa Rosa de Copán are there because they do not fit in. They are the children with crossed eyes and crippled limbs. The children who cannot think quickly.

At this orphanage, there is no money for soap bubbles. The children must rely on the love of strangers to bring them the laughter that everyone says is the best medicine.

It is a medicine not for the twisted bodies the children live in. A medicine not for the clouded minds that struggle to make sense of a world that many of them will never understand.

Laughter is, instead, medicine for the heart.

And the soul.

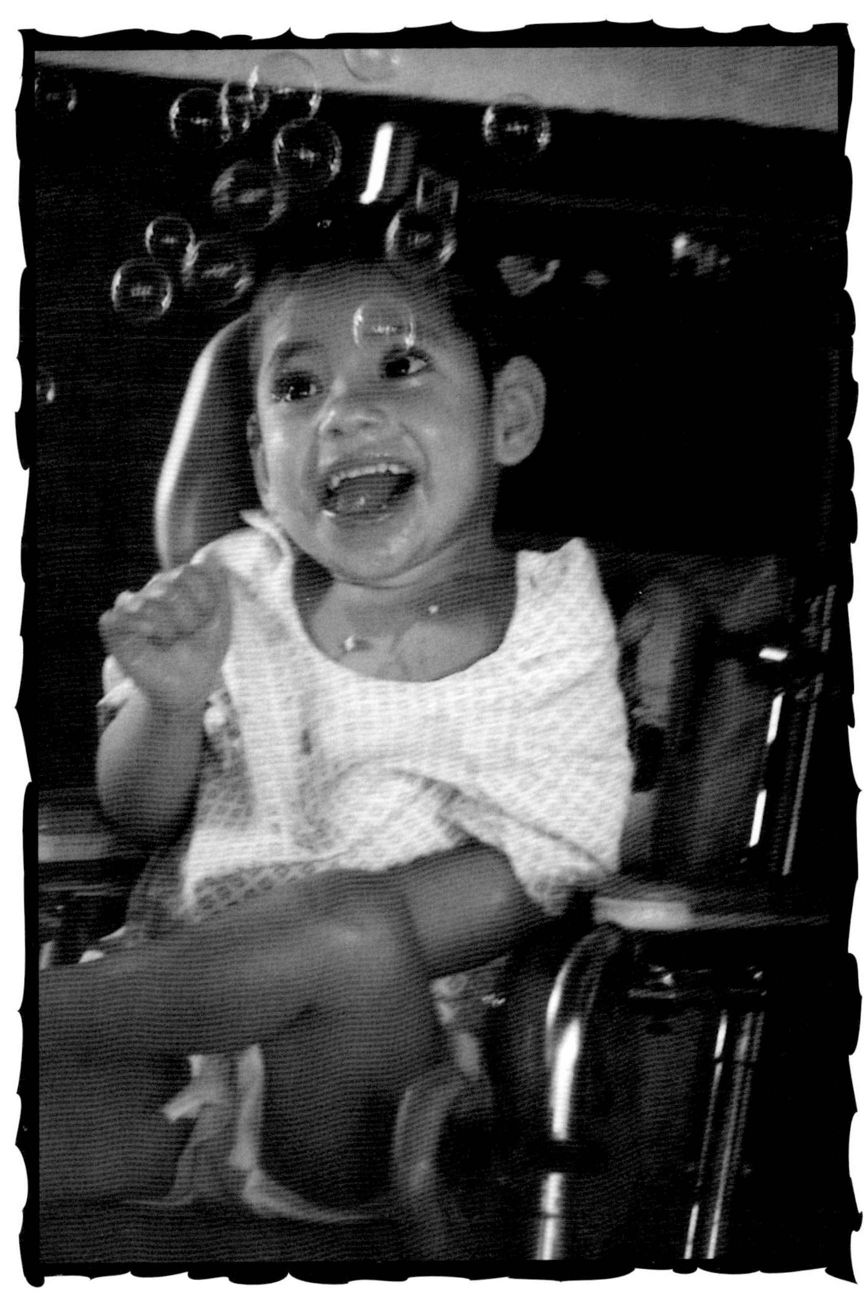

Joy in a Bubble

On the road...

The road was long.

Dusty.

It led to a small village high in the purple mountains where the air is thin.

As thin as the dreams of the people who call that village home.

The dentist made the trip in the back of a truck, sitting near his equipment.

When the bumps threatened to throw him out the back, he just held on more tightly.

In the village he worked a long day, caring for children who had never seen a dentist before.

And through it all, he smiled.

"I can think of no place," he said, "I'd rather be."

The Road Less Traveled

The therapist and the stoic...

He was burned, badly.

But he bore his pain well.

There was a time, not so long ago,

when his burns would have been a life sentence

of pain and poverty.

The therapist worked with him, gently.

Her compassion soothing as her touch.

There was a time, not so long ago,

before the volunteers came,

when she would not have known

just what to do.

That time has passed.

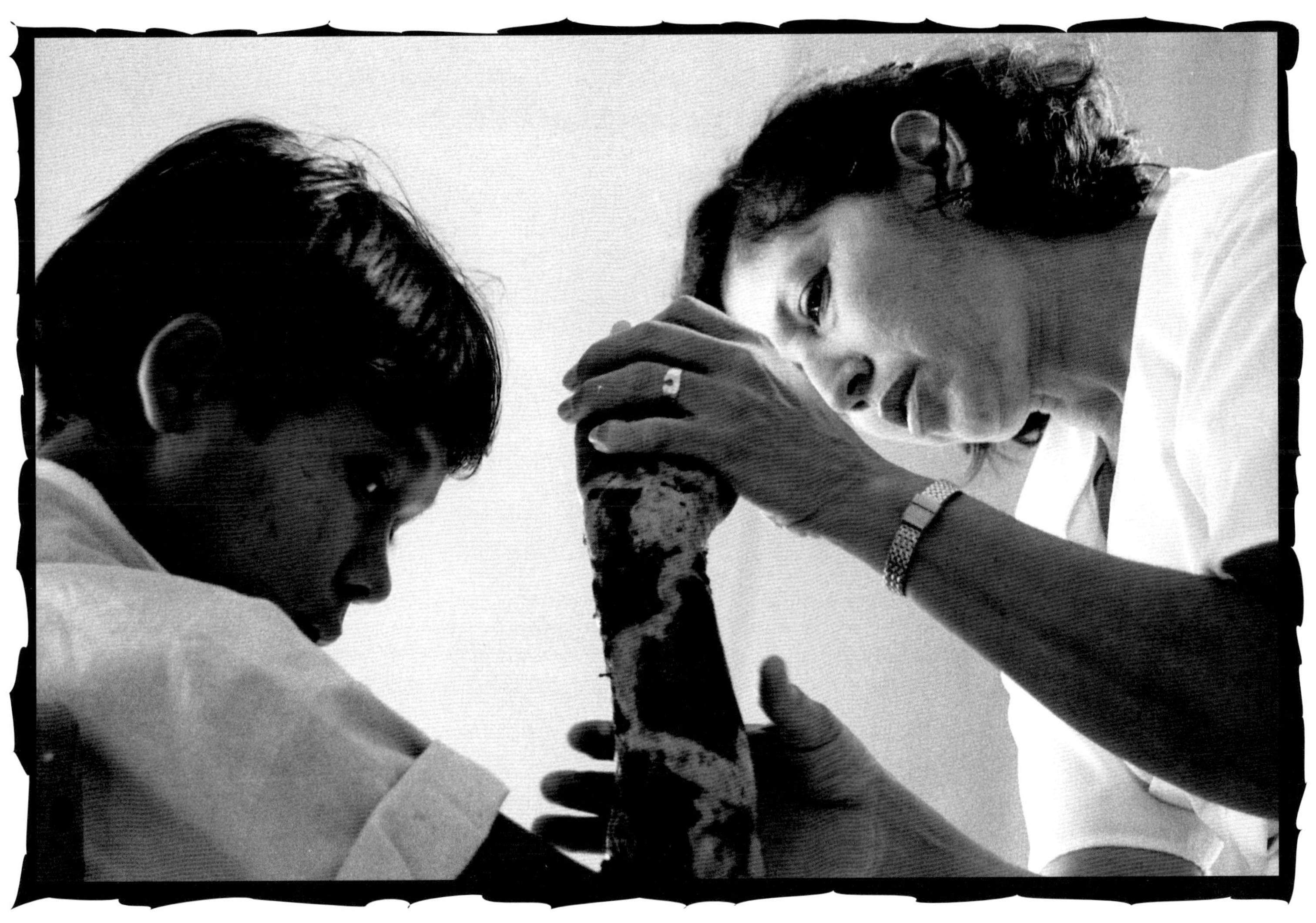

The Therapist and The Stoic

The fruits of our labors...

They have studied, asked questions, and now they have learned new techniques that will one day help them save the life of someone, a child perhaps or an old woman.

And who knows what that might lead to?

Will the child grow up to lead her country? Or become a doctor who will, in turn, save other lives?

Will the old woman teach her grandchildren not to fear people from other lands? Will they then teach that same lesson to their children? Will the planet be more peaceful as a result?

When you drop a pebble into a pond, the ripples spread ever outward until they eventually touch each shore.

The pond is changed forever.

But the change is finite, limited by the earth surrounding the pond.

When you change a life, however, that change is limited only by the cosmos. Who can say what will happen as a result of one act of mercy? One act of kindness? The newly acquired skill of a doctor or nurse?

It is within our power to change lives by educating one another.

And because that is true, it is within our power to change the world.

"By their fruits ye shall know them"
San Pedro Sula, Honduras, C.A.

Gracias, adiós...

It is in the nature of visits that, sooner or later, they must end.

And yet parting need not be sweet sorrow. It need not be full of tears.

At the orphanage in Santa Rosa de Copán, parting is a joyous occasion for the children there. Why? Because they, who have been abandoned by people who should have nurtured them, loved them, and celebrated their lives, understand that the only way someone can leave you is if they first come to see you.

And for them, the fact that someone has spent an hour or two with them is an important gift. It means that someone out there, in that vast, often unpredictable, and sometimes cruel world, loves them simply because they are alive.

So when the volunteers leave, these orphans know that it is not a time for weeping. It is, instead, a time for celebrating the joy of meeting new people.

And celebrating, too, the knowledge that they are important enough for people to journey thousands of miles just to see them.

Adiós!

...and the greatest of these is love

What can I offer?

I am not a doctor, whose skilled hands can pull someone away from the brink of death. I cannot heal the sick nor can I bind up the wounds of violence or mischance.

I am not a nurse. I do not know what to do when a mother whose child is ill looks into my eyes with a silent plea.

I do not understand the workings of the machines that maintain life while the doctors and the nurses work their wonders. I cannot operate those machines nor can I repair them when they fail.

I have no special gifts. No special talents.

What, then, can I offer?

Love.

I can offer love.

I can offer an embrace to a child I do not know. A strong hand to help someone stand who could not stand without that help.

I can be there and, while I cannot heal the sick bodies nor bind the wounds that afflict them, I can offer solace to the souls that inhabit those bodies. I can bring warmth to a heart grown cold from loneliness, light to a life that is in danger of growing dark.

"Love," Stendahl wrote, "is the miracle of civilization."

What, then, can I offer?

Miracles.

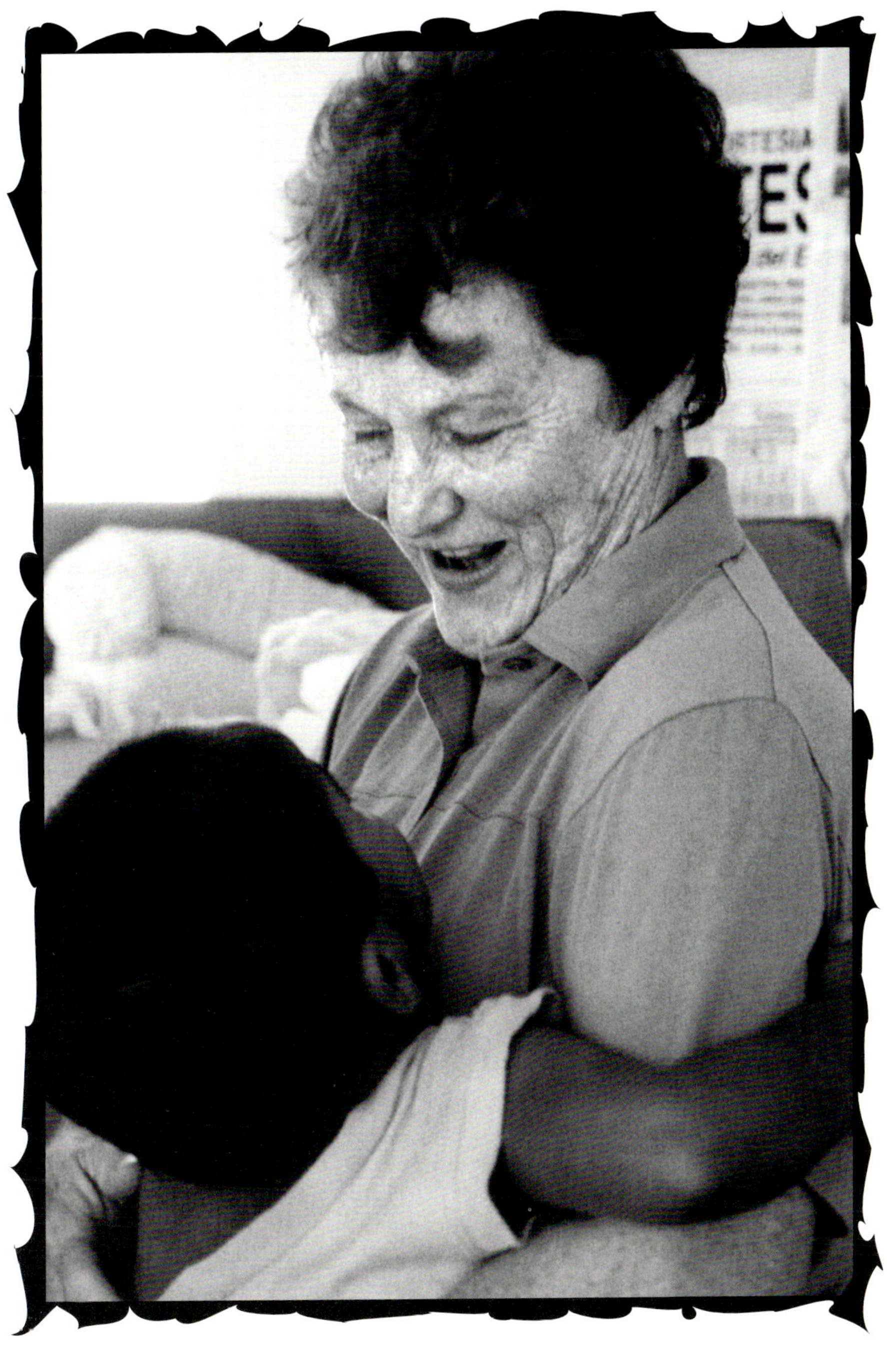

"…and the greatest of these is love"

The long walk...

Though the path be narrow

there is always Someone walking beside you.

Though the path be long, and sometimes treacherous,

Someone is always there.

You can hear His voice whispering in the grass

and feel His breath upon your cheek each time the wind blows.

Those who do God's work know

they are never alone

as they walk the path of life,

living their faith

and doing the Lord's work.

This is the way, walk ye in it.

Isaiah 30:21

CAMO Volunteers

Listed below are the many volunteers from across the United States who have journeyed to the mountains of western Honduras in service to the poor of that country through Central American Medical Outreach (CAMO).

Not listed are the hundreds of stateside volunteers, supporters and donors who collect, repair or donate medical equipment and supplies, help load the four tractor tailor trucks bound for Central America, organize fundraisers to support CAMO efforts, and help with administrative tasks. Without these people, too, CAMO would not be possible.

Abada, Melissa	Wilmington, DE	Prenatal Nurse, '96
Agee, Ruth	Wooster, OH	Registered Physical Therapist, '94, '95
Ahmad, M.D., M	Canton, OH	Plastic Surgeon, '93
Alan, Jane (83)	North Olmsted, OH	Mammography Technologist, '96, '97
Altuna, Brenda	Highland, MI	CRNA, '97
Altuna, Edward (37)(67)	Highland, MI	CRNA, '96, '97
Arney, Kristin	Plymouth, MN	Translator/RPCV, '95, '96, '97
Atkinson, M.D., Scott	East Lansing, MI	Eye Surgeon, '94, '95
Baer, Terry	Canton, OH	Respiratory Therapist, '97
Bartsh, Teresa	Canton, OH	Registered Nurse, '93, '97
Billington, Mike (61)(93)	Wilmington, DE	Journalist, '96, '97
Boron, Mary	Canton, OH	Telephone Installer, '96, '97
Boylan, M.D., Mary	Duluth, MN	Thoracic Surgeon, '94
Breen, Rosemary	Charlottesville, VA	Construction, '97
Bucklen, Kathryn	Raleigh, NC	Translator, '97
Buenaventura, Luz (cover)	Boothwyn, PA	Social Worker, '94, '95
Burky, Bruce	Massillon, OH	Maintenance, '94, '95
Buss, Maxine	Orrville, OH	Dental Assistant, '95
Byrnes, Kathy	Fort Defiance, AZ	Registered Nurse, RPCV, '93, '95, '96, '97
Cress, James	Louisville, OH	Paramedic, '97
Curtiss, M.D., Carl	Canton, OH	Cardiologist, '94
Damm, Ruth	North Canton, OH	Translator, '94
Delong, Michelle	Chicago, IL	Videographer, '94
Demkee, DDS, Donald	Wooster, OH	Dentist, '95
DeSantis, Cari (93)	Hockessin, DE	Administration/Support, '95, '96, '97
Dicks, Allen (71)	Louisville, OH	Biomedical, '94, '95, '96, '97
Dicks, Brian	Louisville, OH	Orphanage, '96
Didrick, D.D.S., Barton (75)	Orrville, Ohio	Dentist, '95
Dillon, Gregory	Charlottesville, VA	Construction, '97
Dillon, Roberta	Charlottesville, VA	Construction, '97
Dolges, Larissa	Orrville, OH	Youth Project, '95
Drew, Greg	Dalton, OH	Youth Project, '95
Dunsieth, Mary	Hummelstown, PA	Registered Nurse, '97
Duran, M.D., Carlos (39)	Greenville, DE	Neonatalogist, '96
Ediger, Erin	Dalton, OH	Youth Project, '95
Foreman, Eva	Southfield, MI	Social Worker, '94, '95
Forte, M.D., Robert (43)	Farmington Hills, MI	Plastic Surgeon, '94, '95, '96
Gaglione, Tammy	Northfield Center, OH	Mammography Technologist, '96
Gerber, Beth	Dalton, OH	Registered Nurse, '94, '95
Gerber, Harley	Dalton, OH	Construction, '94
Gerber, Ted	Dalton, OH	Youth Project, '94, '95
Giles, Marty	Canton, OH	Registered Physical Therapist, '95
Goncalves, Orlando	Canton, OH	Maintenance/Support, '95
Gustafson, DDS, Mark (63)(79)	Wooster, OH	Dentist, '97
Hairston, Tonya	Charlottesville, VA	Construction, '97
Hasseman, Jeremy	Dalton, OH	Youth Project, '95
Hawkins, Rhonda	Canton, OH	Construction, '97
Hernandez, Marion (45)	Newark, DE	Perinatal Resource Mother, '97
Hershberger, Aaron	Dalton, OH	Youth Project, '95
Hershberger, Maxine	Dalton, OH	Youth Project, '94, '95
Himes, Kevin	Dalton, OH	Youth Project, '95
Hirsh, MD, Richard	Akron, OH	Radiologist/Mammography, '96
Hoberman, Liberty	Troy, MI	Plastics, '96
Hoge, Nancy (57)	Bedminster, NJ	Registered Physical Therapist, '95 – '97
Howard, Heidi R	Charlottesville, VA	Construction, '97
Humphrey, M.D., Wendy	North Canton, OH	Obstetrics/Gynecology, '95
Johnson, Joyce	Portland, ME	Registered Nurse - Eyes, 94, '95, '96
Kathol Browne, Ruth (49)	Akron, OH	Mammography Technologist, '97
Keener, Jean	West Salem, OH	Translator, '94, '95, '96
King, Anne	Gallion, OH	Physical Therapy, '94
Knight, Charles	Covesville, VA	Construction, '97
Knight, Laura	Covesville, VA	Construction, '97
Koehler, Beth	Charlottesville, VA	Construction, '97
Lahorra, M.D., John	Cuyahoga Falls, OH	Radiologist/Mammography, '97
Larson, Tim (25)(83)	Canal Fulton, OH	Respiratory Therapy, '95, '96, '97
Lehman, Lesley	Kidron, OH	Youth Project, '95
Leiby, Michele	Louisville, OH	Registered Nurse, '94, '95
Lester, Shawn	Chicago, IL	Videography, '94
Lindeman, Linda (83)	Canton, OH	Mammography Technologist, '97
Lowe, Mevin	Charlottesville, VA	Construction, '97
Manns, Jamie	North Canton, OH	Support, '96
Manns, MD, Robert	Canton, OH	Orthopedic Surgeon, '93, '96, '97
Manuel, Berry	Charlottesville, VA	Construction, '97
McCraw, Frank	Charlottesville, VA	Construction, '97
McFarland, Wanda	Troy, MI	Registered Nurse - Eyes, '94
Miller, Sandra	Kidron, OH	Youth Project, '95
Mina S., Joseph	Ruckersville, VA	Construction, '97
Mohler, Rosalind	Sunbury, OH	Registered Nurse, '97
Mohler M.D., Lester (11)	Sunbury, OH	Plastic Surgeon, '97
Murphy, Joshua (67)	Edinburg, TX	Translator/RPCV, '94,'96, '97
Nemeeth, Garbor	Grosspoint Park, MI	Eyes, '94
Oprea, Michael	Charleston, VA	Registered Nurse, '93, '94
Orr, Rebecca	Charlottesville, VA	Construction, '97
Peterson, Cindy	East Palestine, OH	Ultrasound Technologist, '95
Pycraft, Beth	Wooster, OH	Dental Assistant, '97
Pycraft, M.D., Ronald (59)	Wooster, OH	Eyes, '95, '96, '97
Raber, Mark	Orrville, OH	Construction, '94
Rapp, Michelle	Charlottesville, VA	Construction, '97
Rhoads, DDS, Donald	Orville, OH	Dentist, '95
Riser, Bruce (83)	Charlottesville,VA	Respiratory Therapist, '95, '97
Roberts , David	Charlottesville, VA	Construction, '97
Robeson, DDS, Bruce (51)	Canton, OH	Dentist, '93, '95, '96, '97
Robeson, DDS, Kirk (51)	Canton, OH	Dentist, '97
Robeson, Pat (87)	Canton, OH	Support, '96, '97
Rogers, Mary Lou (43)	Orrville, OH	CRNA, '95
Rogers, DVM, Jack	Orrville, OH	Support, '95
Rossiter, Sarah	Dalton, OH	Youth Project, '95
Rupp, M.D., Dennis	Canton, OH	Cardiologist, '97
Russell, Nancy	Louisville, OH	Registered Nurse, '94, '95, '96, '97
Russell, Robert	Louisville, OH	Support, '97
Schleis, Paula	Akron, OH	Journalist, '96
Schrop, Jerry	Akron, OH	Maintenance, '97
Schwandes, Joanne	Gainesville, FL	Translator/RPCV, '96, '97
Shankle, Cheryl	Canton, OH	Surgical Assistant, '93,'94
Sheets, Amy	Lincoln, NE	Audiologist, '96
Snyder, Beryl	Massillon, OH	Biomedical, '95, '96
Stampone, Ralph (83)	Wilmington, DE	Translator, '96, '97
Stevens, M.D., Andrea	Charlottesville, VA	Pediatrician, '97
Stith, Theresa	East Sparta, OH	Registered Nurse, '95, '96, '97
Stouffer, Bruce	Charlottesville, VA	Construction, '97
Straud, Patricia	Wooster, OH	Audiology, '94, '95, '96
Straud, Steven	Wooster, OH	Audiology, '94, '95, '96
Stubblefield, Jo Mo (Abraham)	Chicago, IL	Videography, '94, '95
Summers, Barbara	Massillon, OH	Support, '95
Swank, Linda	Charlottesville, VA	Construction, '97
Swank, Larry	Charlottesville, VA	Construction, '97
Thomas, Charles	Palmyra, VA	Construction, '97
Thomas, M.D., John (67)	Wooster, OH	Eye Surgeon, '96, '97
Thomas, Judy	Wooster, OH	Support/Eyes, '96, '97
Truitt, M.D., Thomas	Marysville, OH	Eyes, '97
Tschiegg, John	Orrville, OH	Support, '96
Tschiegg, Kathryn (33)(69)	Orrville, OH	Administration/RPCV, '92, '93, '94, '95, '96, '97
Turner, Dietra	Canton, OH	Surgical Assistant, '93
Vaughan Tinus, Mary Ann	Solon, OH	Translator, '94, '95
Vera-Gonzalez, M.D., Anabis (41)	Wilmington, DE	Administration/Translator, '95, '96, '97
Warner, Robert	Uniontown, OH	Biomedical, '94, '95
Wendell, Bill	Noth Canton, OH	Support, '95, '96
Wengerd, Alvin	Apple Creek, OH	Construction, '94
Wheadon, Nancy	Orrville, OH	Registered Nurse/Plastics, '95
Wickwire, Mary Ann	Norton, OH	Registered Nurse/Eyes, '96
Witek, Robin	Akron, OH	Photographer, '96
Wolf, Helane Parnopol	Burmingham, MI	Translator, '94, '95
Wright Sr., Jack	Akron, OH	Support, '96, '97
Zathey, Nancy	Lavonia, MI	Registered Nurse/Plastics, '95, '96
Zurick, M.D., Andrew	Canton, OH	Anesthesiologist, '94

Numbers in parenthesis indicate photo identification

CRNA = Certified Registered Nurse Anesthetist
RPCV = Returned Peace Corps Volunteer

Afterword...

Every journey begins with a single, small step.

But not every journey ends.

For Central American Medical Outreach, that first step was taken many years ago when Kathy Tschiegg first decided to become a Peace Corps volunteer. What forces were at work to send her to Honduras, to a small, overworked mountain hospital? No one knows. Perhaps it is not important that we do know, however, for the important thing is not how she got there but that she got there.

Since that day when she first set foot in the Hospital de Occidente, many others have joined her in that journey. I count myself in that number. Many more will join her in the days and years to come.

There is always room for more people on this trip, for this is truly a journey that has no end in sight. There will always be a need in Santa Rosa de Copán for more medical equipment, for more training, for more love and caring.

There will always be a need for more people to put their faith into action. Some will do so without ever leaving the United States. They will arrange to donate the medical equipment that will save so many more lives there. They will hold fundraisers to help keep this tiny organization running. They will write checks and they will say prayers.

Others will make the trip to Santa Rosa de Copán. They will sacrifice their vacations, pay their own way, work from sun-up to sundown and beyond. They will be doctors, nurses, and dentists. They will be specialists, bio-medical technicians, and people who just want to be of service in any way that they can.

The philosophers have had a lot to say about life down through the ages but, while they may disagree on many fine points, they seem united on this one central truth: Life is sweetest, most meaningful, when you do something for others without thought of recompense of any kind. When you give of yourself, that's when life is itself truly worth the effort it takes to live.

The volunteers who have walked with CAMO on this journey without end have tasted that sweetness. Having tasted it, they have been forever changed by the experience. They are richer because they have helped those who so desperately need helping, and they are better people for having done so.

For them the journey is just beginning, for they have taken that first, small step.

Who is it who will now walk with them along the way?

Mike Billington

About The Writer...

A veteran newspaper reporter and former foreign correspondent for the Fort Lauderdale Sun Sentinel, Mike Billington has covered many of the major news stories of the last half of this century. From upstate New York to South Florida, from Africa's Rwanda, the Saudi Gulf War and a decade of hot politics in the steamy Central American Basin to the domestic battlefields of welfare reform, toxic waste dumps and infant mortality, Mike has seen it all in his nearly thirty years as a journalist.

A published poet, Mike has recently journeyed into the challenging waters of fiction writing with the recent publication of ***Cowboys of the Heart,*** *a trilogy of short stories based loosely on the people he has met and the places he has been during his career. Mike holds a degree in sociology from Ohio's Kent State University. For the past few years, Mike has called Wilmington, Delaware his home.*

About The Photographer...

Cari DeSantis has been photographing people and places for over 20 years, occasionally contributing photos to the many publications she has edited, written or published throughout her two decades working in the communications field. This is the first book to feature such a large body of her photographic work.

An award-winning writer and former magazine editor, Cari has collaborated on a number of books, publications and periodicals over the years, including the history book ***A Legacy from Delaware Women,*** *the art exhibition catalog* ***Four Decades: the Hotel duPont Collection,*** *and the 120,000 circulation quarterly* ***CareLine.*** *Cari is also an avid traveler and noted humanitarian. She holds a bachelors degree in English/journalism, as well as a master of arts degree in liberal studies, both from the University of Delaware. Cari resides in Hockessin, Delaware with her two children.*

Central American Medical Outreach, Inc. (CAMO) is an Ohio-based, Christian-oriented, nonprofit organization dedicated to procuring, distributing and providing medical equipment, supplies and assistance to hospitals and clinics in Third World Central American countries. Through the use of equipment and professional services, CAMO fosters and develops the scientific methods for the diagnosis, prevention and treatment of the Central American population. Within CAMO's program, there thrives a dedication to the promotion of international cooperation and goodwill between the organization and its Third World counterparts. If you would like to learn more about CAMO, please contact Kathyrn Tschiegg, R.N., Executive Director, Central American Medical Outreach, 14821 Burkhart Road, Orrville, Ohio 44667.
Tel: (330) 683-5956. Internet: CAMOKathy@aol.com.